LITTLE BOOK OF THE
OLYMPICS

AN OLYMPIC A to Z

Written by Jon Stroud

LITTLE BOOK OF
OLYMPICS

This edition first published in the UK in 2006
By Green Umbrella

© Green Umbrella Publishing 2006

www.greenumbrella.co.uk

Publishers Jules Gammond, Tim Exell, Vanessa Gardner

Printed and bound in China

ISBN-13: 978-1-905009-93-0
ISBN-10: 1-905009-93-3

Contents

Amsterdam 1928

ABOVE Competitors clearing the first set of hurdles at the 1928 Games

BELOW The parade at the opening ceremony of the 1928 Olympics

A FEELING OF PEACE AND RECONciliation was present at the Amsterdam Games of 1928 as Germany was once again permitted to attend. The tradition of the parade of nations was continued from the 1924 Paris Games but, on this occasion, it would be Greece who would march in first with the Dutch team last. This protocol – Greece first, host nation last – remains to this day.

One of the great symbols of the Games, the Olympic flame, was lit for the first time.

Japanese triple jumper Mikio Oda became the first Asian athlete to win an individual Olympic gold medal. Within a week compatriot Yoshiyuki Tsuruta would take gold in the 200m breaststroke with a new Olympic record of 2:48.8. Not to be outdone India claimed victory in the field hockey starting a winning run that would see them through to the 1960 Rome Games.

136 female athletes had competed in the 1924 Paris Games but with the inclusion of women's gymnastics and track and field, the Amsterdam games saw this number increase to 290. When, in the final of the women's 800m, several athletes collapsed to the ground the male dominated I.A.A.F. seized the opportunity and banned all women's races over 200m. It would be 32 years before women would compete at a greater distance in the Olympic Games.

Antwerp 1920

THE 1920 GAMES, HELD IN ANTWERP to honour the suffering of the Belgian nation during the First World War, saw 22 nations represented. Germany, Austria, Bulgaria, Hungary and Turkey, all considered aggressor nations, were excluded. In addition Russia was an absentee as its troops were fighting the civil war.

The opening ceremony would herald two important additions to Olympic tradition; the Olympic flag, its five rings inspired by the altar at Delphi representing unity of the five continents, and the Olympic oath.

"In the name of the competitors, I promise that we shall take part in these Olympic Games, representing and abiding by the rules that govern them, in the true spirit of sportsmanship for the glory of the sport and the honour of our teams."

The 1920 Games would see a number of outstanding performances. Tennis player Suzanne Lenglen of France won two gold medals and a bronze losing only four games in ten sets of singles play. Italy's Nedo Nadi achieved a feat as yet unequalled by winning gold medals in five of the six fencing events. At 72 years old, Oscar Swahn of Sweden, previously having won a gold medal at the 1908 Games, took silver in the team double-shot running deer competition to become the oldest Olympic medallist ever.

ABOVE Suzanne Lenglen competing in the women's tennis tournament

Aquatics

THERE ARE FOUR AREAS OF OLYMPIC competition referred to as aquatics; swimming, diving, water polo and synchronised swimming.

The first Olympic swimming events took place at the inaugural Athens Games of 1896 in the open waters of the Bay of Zea on a course marked out by floating hollowed-out pumpkins. Hungarian Alfréd Hajós, inspired to take up swimming following the death by drowning of his father, became the first Olympic swimming Champion, winning the 100 metres freestyle in 1:22.2. A more unusual swimming event was the 100 metres freestyle for sailors which, not surprisingly, received a limited number of entries.

An expanded swimming program at the 1900 Games in Paris, produced a series of incredibly fast times influenced largely by the fact that they were swum in the River Seine with the assistance of the currant. Events included a 200 metre obstacle race and underwater swimming where marks were awarded dependant on time and distance.

Women's events were introduced at the 1912 Stockholm Games with a limited competition consisting of the 200 metres freestyle and 4x100 metres relay. It was not until the 1924 Paris Olympics that a wider selection of events was launched.

Olympic swimming events are no longer held in the open sea or fast flowing rivers! An Olympic pool must be 50 metres in length with eight marked lanes. Competitors are required to swim preliminary qualifiers. In events of 400 metres or over, the eight fastest qualifiers advance to the final whilst in

shorter events 16 qualifiers then compete in a semi-final with eight then going forward. The fastest qualifiers are then placed in the centre lanes of the pool for the final as these experience less water turbulence than those at the edges.

Rules governing false starts differ to those in athletics events. For a first false start no competitor is penalised in any way but in subsequent false starts the offending swimmer is automatically disqualified, whether they were guilty of the first false start or not.

Diving events always attract a great deal of interest at the Olympic Games. There are two forms of competition, springboard diving and platform diving, contested individually and as synchronised pairs with events for both men and women.

In springboard diving competitors dive from a flexible board no less than 4.8 metres long and 0.5 metres wide fixed three metres above the water whilst platform diving is performed from a rigid platform at least six metres long and two metres wide suspended

BELOW Hungarian Tibor Benedek (R) vies with Alexandar Sapic (L) and Vladimir Vujasinovic from Serbia Montenegro during the men's gold medal match at the Olympic aquatic center at the 2004 Olympic Games in Athens

10 meters above the water. Seven judges score each dive with the result being multiplied by a difficulty coefficient that reflects the complexity of the dive performed.

Water polo is a tough physical sport played between two teams of 13 players although only seven players including the goalkeeper are in the water at any one time. The game is played over 28 minutes split into four 7 minute quarters within a field of play 30 metres by 20 metres. The object is to score a goal by putting the ball between the posts of the opponent's goal. The ball may be played with any part of the body except a clenched fist. In Olympic competition men's and women's medals are contested in separate tournaments.

Synchronised swimming, seen by some as a rather trivial sport, is in fact incredibly demanding both physically and mentally with athletes expected to combine strength, stamina and ballet like grace. Olympic synchronised swimming takes the form of a pair's competition and a team event for teams of eight swimmers. In each discipline two routines are performed. The first is a technical routine comprising set manoeuvres, the second is a free routine where the creativity and choreography of the swimmers is put to the test both being scored by a panel of five judges.

Athens 1896

"I declare the opening of the first international Olympic Games in Athens. Long live the Nation. Long live the Greek people."

WITH AN ESTIMATED 80,000 SPECtators filling Athens' newly restored Panathenic stadium and most of the 245 competing athletes arranged by the 14 nations they represented filling the infield, these words, uttered by King George I of Greece, heralded the opening of the Games of the First Olympiad. The date was 6 April 1896.

The first competition of the inaugural games was the opening heats of the 100 metre dash. The American athletes proved outstanding with Frank Lane of Princetown recording a time of 12.2 seconds in that initial round with quarter mile specialists Thomas Burke and Thomas Curtis taking the subsequent two with identical times of 12.0 seconds. The "unusual" crouched start of these two Bostonians caused much interest with the European audience. Four days later it would be Burke who took victory in the final by 2 metres

from Germany's Fritz Hofmann once again recording 12.0 seconds.

The honour of becoming the first Olympic Champion since the 369AD victory of Armenian boxer Prince Varasdates fell to another Bostonian. Born to a poor Irish-American family,

BELOW The Olympic stadium in Athens, 1896

the 27 year old self–educated Harvard freshman and US triple jump champion James Connolly outdistanced popular Frenchman Alexandre Tuffère by over a metre. What should have been a wonderful moment of triumph for the young American was somewhat tainted by the crowds frosty reception to his endeavours. Having dominated the preceding 100 metre heats the Americans were not the flavour of choice for the partisan Greek spectators.

Greek honour was to be restored by the marathon efforts of farmer Spiridon Louis who later revealed that whilst completing his military service a year earlier as groom to the horses of General Mavromichalis, he had been inspired to competition when shown the finish line of the uncompleted Olympic stadium. To the delight of the 100,000 crowd the diminutive figure of this Greek athlete emerged through the white marble gates of the Panathenic stadium in first place. Rapturous applause followed as Prince George and Crown Prince Constantine ran to his side urging him to the finish where an overjoyed King George stood waiting. Louis's time of 2:58:50 was over seven minutes faster than second placed compatriot Charilaos Vasilakos.

It would be another 108 years before the games would return to Athens in their official form although the enthusiastic Greeks organised an Intercalated (intermediary) Games in 1906. A 1949 commission of the IOC declared that these games were wholly unofficial with the matter remaining closed since.

BELOW The start of the 100 metres sprint at the first Olympic Games of the Modern Era in Athens

Athens 2004

AFTER LEADING IN ALL VOTING rounds, Athens was finally chosen to host the 2004 Olympic Games on 5 September 1997. The Olympics were coming home. An ambitious program of construction was devised with the intention of constructing state-of-the-art stadiums and, crucially, improving Athens aging transport infrastructure.

To the watching world it seemed that the Greeks would not finish the project on time as construction appeared shockingly slow. Even by late March 2004, with the Games just five months away, some developments were still behind schedule. The main Olympic stadium was finally completed with just two months to spare.

Controversy struck the Games even before they had opened. Greek Olympic 200m Champion Kostas Kenderis had been selected to light the Olympic flame at the opening ceremony but, just days before the Games commenced, Kenderis and women's 100 metre silver medallist Katerina Thanou missed a random drug test subsequently claiming that they had been involved in a motorcycle accident. No record exists of such an accident and neither athlete competed in Athens.

Despite these early setbacks, the Games were a resounding success. 11,099 athletes from 202 countries participated in 301 events across 28 sports.

American Michael Phelps dominated the men's swimming events collecting six gold and two bronze medals to become only the second man to win eight medals at one Olympic Games. If Phelps were a country he would have

BELOW A bronze statue of a discus thrower stands outside the all-marble Panathenaic stadium with the Olympic rings in the background

come sixteenth in the medal tables beating Spain, Canada and New Zealand.

In other waterborne competitions, German Canoeist Birgit Fischer became the second athlete in the history of the Games to win gold medals at six different Olympics. British yachtsman Ben Ainslie won his second gold medal in the Laser class following his success at Sydney whilst compatriot Matthew Pinsent won his fourth consecutive rowing gold medal.

Popular British athlete Kelly Holmes completed an astounding double taking victory in both the 800 and 1500 metre finals but the weight of expectation hung heavy around the neck of fellow Briton Paula Radcliffe who, suffering from heat exhaustion and the effects of a stomach bug, was forced to pull out of the women's marathon with just five

miles to go. Moroccan Hicham El Guerrouj achieved an exciting double winning a gold medal in the 1500 metres and the 5000 metres.

A dramatic men's marathon saw Brazilian Vanderlei de Lima accosted by a spectator whilst leading the race. Visibly shaken, de Lima was subsequently passed by Italian Stefano Baldini, to finish in third place. For demonstrating fair play de Lima was awarded the Pierre de Coubertin medal at the closing ceremony.

Having shown promise in Sydney, the British track cycling team made their mark at the Athens Games with Bradley Wiggins collecting three medals, one of each colour, and Scotland's Chris Hoy winning a gold medal in the 1km time trial.

Atlanta 1996

IT SEEMED A LOGICAL, FOREGONE conclusion that the centenary Games would be awarded to Athens, the spiritual home of the Olympics and site of the first modern Games. However, a different logic prevailed. With American corporations providing so much capital investment through rights revenues the IOC voted in favour of Atlanta by 51 votes to 35.

In spite of some outstanding performances the 1996 Atlanta Olympics will always be regarded as flawed. Organisation of the Games was extremely poor. Atlanta's creaking transport infrastructure failed to cope with the demands of the thousands of visiting athletes and spectators whilst an outdated computerised results system constantly broke down. Inadequately trained volunteer staff added to the confusion. There were many complaints of commercial exploitation directed at the Centennial Olympic Park. This location would gain further notoriety on 27 July as a bomb exploded killing one person and injuring 110. Amazingly the Park had not been included in the Games security system.

In an emotional display, and in the presence of a record 10,310 athletes from 197 nations, the Olympic flame was lit by the frail boxing legend Muhammad Ali who, as Cassius Clay, had won an Olympic light-heavyweight gold medal in 1960.

Carl Lewis of the United States, competing at his fourth Olympics, once again took the gold medal in the long

BELOW Former heavyweight boxing Champion and 1960 Olymplc gold medallist Muhammad Ali lights the flame during the opening ceremony at the Olympic Stadium in Atlanta

jump to become only the third person to have won the same individual event on four occasions. In doing so Lewis took his career tally to nine Olympic gold medals.

BELOW An aerial view of the Olympic stadium in Atlanta

With his unique upright action and gold running spikes, America's Michael Johnson became the athletic icon of the games. Johnson, the reigning world record holder over 400m was last out of the blocks in the Olympic final but quickly recovered storming into the lead after 300m and pulling away to win by four metres in 43.84 seconds. In a truly outstanding performance, Johnson demolished his own 200m world record by 0.34 seconds with a time of 19.32 seconds finishing four metres clear of silver medallist Frankie Fredericks. Timing revealed Johnson had run the last 100m in 9.20 seconds.

French star Marie-José Pérec emulated Johnson's double by taking the 200m and 400m gold medals in the women's events. In taking the 200m/400m double, both Pérec and Johnson had achieved a feat never before seen at the Olympic games in un-boycotted competition.

A more unusual record was broken by Austrian yachtsman Hubert Raudaschl who became the first competitor to have competed in nine Olympic Games.

Barcelona 1992

DURING THE INTERVENING YEARS between the 1988 Seoul Games and those of Barcelona in 1992 the global map had changed almost beyond recognition. The Berlin Wall had fallen and Germany was once again a reunified nation. In South Africa the Apartheid system had come to an end. Communism had collapsed in the Soviet Union with the USSR being split into 15 individual countries.

As Spanish archery Paralympian Antonio Rebollo launched a flaming arrow to light the Olympic flame, the Games of the XXV Olympiad opened with all nations present for the first time in 20 years with the ex-communist republics competing as the Unified Team. Having taken military action against Croatia and Bosnia-Herzegovina, Yugoslavia was banned from international competition but its individual ath-

letes were given permission to compete as "Independent Olympic Participants".

BELOW Fireworks during the closing ceremony

RIGHT Forward Karl Malone of the United States goes up for two during a game against Germany at the Olympic Games in Barcelona

BELOW All around individual gymnast gold medalist Vitaly Scherbo from Unified team (Belarus), shows his gold medal to the public

For the first time the men's basketball competition was opened to professional athletes. Known as "The Dream Team", the United States fielded a squad including NBA stars Michael Jordan, Larry Bird, Magic Johnson and Charles Barclay. Averaging 117 points per game the American team never called a time-out in the entire tournament, defeating Croatia 85-117 to take the gold medal.

The young Belarusian gymnast Vitaly Scherbo had been described by his coach, Aleksandr Arkeyev, as "a showman". Arkeyev's point was to be proven as Scherbo dominated his opposition winning the parallel bar, long horse vault, rings, pommel horse, team combined and all-round competition to take six gold medals, four of these on a single day. Only the great swimmer Mark Spitz has won more gold medals at a single Olympiad.

At 32 years old, Great Britain's Linford Christie achieved a lifetime ambition by beating Namibian Frankie Fredericks and Dennis Mitchell of the United States to become the oldest ever winner of the men's 100m final. The women's 100m final was equally exciting with Gail Devers taking victory with only six hundredths of a second

separating the first five athletes.

On a different kind of track, Britain's Chris Boardman pedalled his way to victory in the 4000m cycling pursuit final. In an event where the result is often determined by hundredths of a second, Boardman achieved the unthinkable and actually lapped his opponent Jens Lehman. Much hype was centred on Boardman's carbon-fibre Lotus designed cycle but defeated Lehman insisted he had been beaten by the man and not by the bike.

Popular Italian Fabio Casartelli took victory in the cycling road race. Tragically Casartelli died of his injuries after crashing on the decent of the Portet-d'Aspet during the 1999 Tour de France.

Barefoot Abebe Bikila

AS ARGENTINEAN JUAN CARLOS Zabala completed the marathon course of the 1932 Los Angeles Games in an Olympic record time of 2:31 36 thousands of miles away in the town of Mout, Ethiopia, a child was born. His name was Abebe Bikila.

The Ethiopian government had employed Swede Onni Niskanen to take charge of the nation's physical education. Part of his remit was to supervise the training of Emperor Haile Selassie's personal bodyguard. It was here that Niskanen discovered Bikila as a young soldier with immense stamina. Seeing his potential, Niskanen took to preparing Bikila for the marathon. Training in the mountains around Addis Ababa, often twice a day and always barefoot, he easily qualified for the 1960 Rome Olympics.

The marathon in Rome was the first to be run at night. With Italian soldiers lighting the course with torches, barefoot Bikila and the race favourite, Moroccan Rhandi Ben Abdesselem,

LEFT Ethiopian athlete Abebe Bikila runs barefoot for victory in the Rome 1960 Olympic Games marathon

broke away after 18 kilometres. The two athletes ran side by side until they reached the obelisk of Axum; an Ethiopian relic that had been looted by Italian troops. With less than a mile to go Bikila attacked, quickly putting ground into his opponent he crossed the line in 2:15:16.2 to set a new world record by just over a minute. In doing so Bikila had become the first black African to win an Olympic Gold medal.

Despite having undergone an appendectomy only 40 days prior to the race, Bikila successfully defended his title at the 1964 Tokyo Games, again setting a new world record.

Beijing 2008

THE CHINESE CAPITAL, BEIJING, was elected to host the Games of the XXIX Olympiad by the International Olympic Committee in July 2001 after defeating Istanbul, Osaka, Paris and Toronto in the final rounds of voting. The Games will open at 8pm on 8 August 2008 (8:00, 08-08-08), the number eight being considered a symbol of prosperity in Chinese culture. It is estimated that 10,500 athletes will attend accompanied by 20,000 accredited media personnel.

In selecting a host city the IOC emphasises a need to create a sustainable legacy, not just in sporting terms but in infrastructure that will be of benefit to the local communities. With this in mind the Beijing organising committee have embarked on an extensive development program with 11 new competition venues being constructed and 11 existing venues being completely renovated.

Central to the project are the exciting new National Stadium, National Aquatics Centre and National Indoor Stadium. All of these projects are situated within the Olympic Green, an extensive area of parkland and woods that incorporates areas of wetlands, meadows and upland forests. The 91,000 seat Stadium, an exciting creation of steel, will host the opening and closing ceremonies and the athletics competitions. Originally designed to incorporate a sliding roof this part of the project has now been omitted in an attempt to reduce spiralling construction costs.

The 17,000 seat Aquatic Centre, known as the Water Cube takes on the stunning appearance of being con-

BELOW Workers at the construction site of the National Olympic Stadium in Beijing, China. The main body of the Stadium has been dubbed the "bird nest" because of its unique design

structed from bubbles. The Indoor Stadium, home of the gymnastics and handball tournaments, will take on a life as a cultural and entertainment venue after the close of the Games.

Five venues outside of Beijing will host events in 2008. It was announced in July 2005 that the equestrian events would be contested in Hong Kong due to the issues regarding quarantine and the difficulties in establishing a disease free zone in the city. Tianjin, Shanghai and Qinhuangdao will all host preliminary rounds of the football competition. The sailing events will be hosted at a newly constructed

venue in Qingdao, a city on the southern coast of the Shandong Peninsula.

A total of 302 medal events, 165 for men and 127 for women, will be contested across 28 sports at the 2008 Beijing Games. New events announced for the Beijing Games include the women's 3,000 metres steeplechase,

women's foil and sabre team events, men's and women's marathon 10,000 metres swimming and the replacement of the table tennis doubles with a team event. In addition an entirely new discipline will be introduced in the cycling category with the inclusion of men's and women's BMX racing.

ABOVE Participators hold the Olympic rings as they take part in a folk dance competition aimed at promoting sporting activities as Beijing gears up to host the 2008 Olympics

Berlin 1936

IT WAS CLEAR THAT THE NATURE of the Berlin Games of 1936 would be like no other. Prior to the opening an inaugural torch relay had taken place where a lighted torch was carried from the Olympia to Berlin – another institution which lives on in Olympic tradition to this day. Adolf Hitler had decided that the Olympics would be an ideal platform from which to demonstrate the racial superiority of the Aryan people. With a well prepared team of exceptional athletes, 4.5 million tickets sold and the world's press in attendance it seemed that he might be proved right.

The crack German squad would take 33 gold medals, a vast improvement of the three they collected at Los Angeles in 1932. With images beamed directly onto 28 big screens located about Berlin, the stage was set for Teutonic dominance. But it would be the efforts of African-American athletes Ralph Metcalf, John Woodruff, Cornelius Johnson and Jesse Owens that would take the headlines of the newspapers and the hearts of the devotees the world over.

MIDDLE Aerial view of the Olympic stadium (background) and the Olympic swimming pool

BELOW Konrad von Wangenheim with his arm in a sling, shortly before riding 'Kurfurst' in the three day team event

Sprinter and long-jumper Owens appeared as the undoubted hero of the Games taking gold medals in the 100m, 200m, long jump and the 4x100m relay. It was reported that, after Owens' victory in the long jump, Hitler refused to offer his congratulations as the athlete did not conform to the Reich Chancellor's view of racial superiority. Owens has since discounted these accounts claiming that he was well treated by the Germans during his stay.

Diminutive Marjorie Gestring from Los Angeles, at just 13 years old, became

the youngest ever Olympic gold medallist by taking victory in the women's springboard diving whilst Inge Sorrenson, representing Denmark, set another record by becoming the Games youngest ever individual medallist taking bronze in the 200 metre breaststroke at the age of 12.

Incredible personal sacrifice was seen in the actions of Lieutenant Konrad von Wangenheim, a member of the German equestrian three-day event team. A heavy fall in the steeplechase element broke von Wangenheim's collar bone but, knowing that his failure to finish would result in the disqualification of the German team, he remounted and completed the course. The following day, this time during the show jumping element, von Wangenheim was again unseated as his horse, Kurfürst, reared and fell upon him. At first onlookers feared he had been killed but he jumped to his feet and remounted to complete the remainder of the course without a fault taking Germany to a much deserved team gold medal.

Black Power

RIGHT American track and field athletes Tommie Smith and John Carlos, first and third place winners in the 200 metre race, protest with the Black Power salute as they stand on the winner's podium

AT THE 1968 MEXICO CITY GAMES, two Americans were expected to dominate the 200 metres. Tommie Smith was the holder of 11 world indoor and outdoor records whilst John Carlos had beaten Smith at the U.S. Olympic trials. Both athletes were students at San Jose State College and were members of the Olympic Project for Human Rights, a campaigning organisation that sought to highlight the treatment of blacks in the United States.

The final was dramatic as an in-form Smith streaked passed his team mate to take a decisive victory and a new world record. Carlos, transfixed on Smith as he charged to the tape, failed to see Australian Peter Norman slip past to take the silver medal and was relegated to the bronze.

The real drama enfolded at the medal ceremony where, in memorial to black Americans who had been lynched, the black athletes mounted the podium barefoot with Smith wearing a black scarf around his neck and Carlos a string of beads. In solidarity, Australian silver medallist Norman wore a civil right movement badge. As The Star Spangled Banner played, Smith and Carlos each raised a gloved fist and bowed their heads.

The IOC was outraged, demanding that Smith and Carlos should be banned from Olympic competition. Initially the U.S. Olympic Committee refused to comply but the threat of the entire US track & field team being excluded forced their hand. Smith and Carlos were banned from the Olympic Village and sent home to the United States.

Beamon

FORCED TO TRAIN WITHOUT A coach due to a suspension, 22 year old Bob Beamon's preparations for the 1968 Mexico City Games were far from ideal. Despite the presence of all three medal winners from the 1964 Tokyo Games, Beamon was considered the favourite having won 22 out of his last 23 meetings.

In the qualification round Beamon almost ended up with an early plane ticket home as he fouled twice. 1964 silver medallist Ralph Boston offered some advice, suggesting that he should make a mark before the take-off board and aim for that just as Jesse Owens had done in 1936. Beamon made the mark and qualified easily.

The night before the Olympic final, Beamon changed his preparation in a major way. Rather than resting and recuperating he engaged in sexual intercourse. All at once he was convinced he had blown his chances.

Seventeen athletes had qualified for the final but the first three jumpers fouled leaving a nervous Beamon to post the first distance of the competition. He sprinted down the runway, hit the board perfectly and glided high through the air. Attempting to calculate his jump the officials found their special measuring device to be too short. Beamon had jumped an incredible 8.90 metres and in doing so had set a new world record by 55 centimetres - a record that would last for 22 years 316 days.

BELOW Bob Beamon of the USA breaking the Long Jump World Record during the 1968 Olympic Games in Mexico City

Boardman

THE IMAGE OF CHRIS BOARDMAN astride the Lotus "super-bike", powering his way to victory is one of the icons of British Olympic achievement. Great Britain went to the 1992 Barcelona Olympics in the knowledge that its last cycling gold medals had been awarded to Harry Ryan and Thomas Lance in 1920.

Media attention was drawn to the relatively unknown Boardman after his first round qualification time was posted.

Recording 4:27.327 he had taken an astonishing four seconds off the world record time of reigning Olympic Champion Gintautas Umaras. The following evening Boardman rode his quarter-final against Jan-Bo Petersen of Denmark. Storming home in 4:24.496, he lowered the record by another three seconds despite easing up in the final lap having caught his opponent.

In the semi-final, with a win rather than a time being of importance, Boardman eased himself into a lead over New Zealander Gary Anderson, stayed there to record a relatively slow 4:29.332, guaranteeing him a ride in the final.

The final pitched Boardman against Germany's World Champion Jens Lehman. Powering smoothly away from the start, Boardman was already in the lead after one lap. Approaching the halfway distance Lehman's deficit was increased to three seconds, an insurmountable distance to close in a pursuit race. Finally, with one lap remaining, he caught Lehman and secured the gold medal.

With the media giving as much credit to the Lotus bicycle as to Boardman, Lehman graciously insisted he had been beaten by the rider and not the bike.

BELOW Chris Boardman of Great Britain in action on his Lotus Superbike during the 4000 metres Individual Pursuit final in the Velodrome at the 1992 Olympics in Barcelona

Blankers-Koen

THE DAUGHTER OF A DUTCH farmer, Francina "Fanny" Koen took up competitive sport at the age of 14, quickly proving herself to be a true all-round athlete. At 18, under the guidance of triple jumper Jan Blankers, she qualified for the 1936 Berlin Olympics. Despite tying for sixth place in the high jump and finishing fifth in the 4x100 metres relay, her highlight of the games was acquiring Jesse Owens' autograph.

In the intervening years between the Games, Koen became the first woman to run 100 yards in 11.0 seconds and the holder of five other world records. Early in 1940 she had become engaged to her coach, Jan Blankers. Marrying in August 1940 she took the name Francina Blankers-Koen.

As the 1948 Olympics approached it seemed inconceivable that this 30 year old housewife, now a mother of two, would be competitive despite her world records. Blankers-Koen proved the doubters wrong.

First she took a decisive victory in the 100 metres with a time of 11.9 second. Having openly dismissed Blankers-Koen, British 200 metre runner Audrey Wilson was then humiliated, trailing 6 metres behind the triumphant Dutch sprinter. A new world record was set in the 80 metres hurdles – the only track world record of the 1948 Games. Finally, starting her leg of the 4x100 metres trailing in fourth place, she pulled her team back to take her fourth Olympic gold medal of the games.

BELOW Fanny Blankers-Koen crosses the finishing line of the 200m event, at Wembley stadium, where she captured four gold medals, 100m, 200m, 80m hurdles and 4x100

Biondi

RIGHT Matt Biondi of the USA in action during the 1988 Olympic Games in Seoul, South Korea

BELOW US swimmer Matt Biondi celebrates under the Olympic rings after he won gold in the 100m freestyle during the 1988 Olympics

HAVING ALREADY GAINED an Olympic gold medal as part of the all conquering 4x 100 metre freestyle team at the Los Angeles Olympics, the achievements of American Matt Biondi at the 1988 Seoul Olympic Games were nothing short of astounding.

Biondi's first opportunity to shine was in the final of the 200 metres freestyle. With a strong field including Germany's world record holder Michael Gross, Biondi was dominant for the first 150 metres. He had not though counted upon Australian Duncan Armstrong who, placed in the adjacent lane, had in his own words, "bodysurfed the first 100 metres" in Biondi's wake. With 25 metres to go Armstrong stormed away to take victory relegating a stunned Biondi into third place.

Two days later it looked as if Biondi's luck would not change. With just 10 metres to go in the 100 metres butterfly he misjudged his finishing kick and stalled in the water allowing Anthony Nesty of Suriname to take victory by one hundredth of a second.

Biondi's luck turned that afternoon as he took his first gold medal of the Games swimming the tail leg of the 4x200 metres freestyle relay and recording a world record in the process. Biondo went on to win one gold medal a day for the next four days, setting three further world and four Olympic records in the process and taking victory in the 50 metres and 100 metres freestyle, 4x100 metres freestyle relay and 4x100 metres medley.

Čáslavská

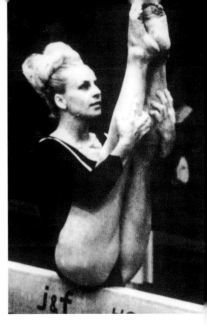

CZECH GYMNAST VĚRA ČÁSLAVSKÁ was born in Prague in May 1942. Originally a figure skater, Čáslavská took easily to the grace, balance and physical demands of gymnastics. A 1958 World Championship team silver medal in her debut international competition gave an indication of the greatness to come, a feat she repeated at her first Olympics, the 1960 Games in Rome.

A second Olympic appearance at the 1964 Games proved to the world what a dominant force the young Czech had become. Gold medals in the individual all-round competition, horse-vault and balance beam plus a silver medal in the team event made Čáslavská the most successful female gymnast of the Games.

Věra Čáslavská's fame reached its peak at the 1968 Mexico City Olympics. Two months before the Games, Soviet troops had crossed the border into Czechoslovakia forcing Čáslavská, an outspoken supporter of the democratic movement, to go into hiding. Granted permission to attend the Games at the last minute, she once again dominated the gymnastics competition taking gold medals in the individual all-round, floor, asymmetric bars and the horse vault and silver medals for the team all-round and the balance beam.

Čáslavská complemented her gold medals with a gold ring, marrying her fiancé, Czech 1500 metres runner Josef Odložil, in a ceremony at the Games. Perhaps inspired by her use of "Jarabe tapatío" – the Mexican Hat Dance – for her floor exercise, 10,000 well wishers attended the wedding.

ABOVE Czech Věra Čáslavská performs her routine on the beam at the Olympic Games in Mexico,1968

Christie

LINFORD CHRISTIE HAS enjoyed a mixed reputation. Born in Saint Andrew, Jamaica in 1960, he emigrated at the age of seven to join his parents in Britain. Only when 19 years old did Christie develop an interest in competitive athletics.

Although showing early promise, Christie failed in selection for the 1984 Los Angeles Games. Under the coaching of Ron Roddan, his performances gradually improved until, to the surprise of many, he won the 100 metres at the 1986 European Championships.

Christie qualified easily for the final of the 100 metres at Seoul in 1988. Bursting out of the blocks, his piercing gaze fixed on the finishing line, Christie charged down the track. Two athletes finished ahead of him; Canadian Ben Johnson and American Carl Lewis. Johnson, testing positive for the steroid stanozolol, was subsequently stripped of his gold medal elevating Christie to silver. Christie himself tested positive for the stimulant pseudoephedrine but

RIGHT Linford Christie raises his arms as he crosses the line to win the 100 metres final at the 1992 Olympic Games

BELOW Linford Christie acknowledges the cheers of the crowd during the medal ceremony for the 100 metres at the Olympic Games in Barcelona

the amount was so small that no action was taken.

At the 1992 Barcelona Olympics Christie truly made his mark on the Games. Now 32 years old, he was in the best form of his life. Canadian Bruny Surin took an early lead with Namibian Frankie Fredericks in second place but Christie stormed past them both to become the oldest male athlete to win the Olympic 100 metres title.

The 1996 Atlanta Games were less successful for Christie. False-starting twice he was disqualified by track referee John Chaplin. Fiery as ever, Christie left the track, albeit reluctantly, throwing his running spikes into a rubbish bin.

Comăneci

IT CAN SEEM STRANGE THAT AN event as huge as the Olympic Games can be dominated by someone so tiny but that is exactly what happened at the 1976 Montreal Games when 4 foot 10 inch, 14 year old, Romanian Nadia Comăneci stepped into the limelight.

Born in Onești in 1961, Comăneci had begun competing in gymnastics at the age of six representing her home town. Coached by Bela Karolyi, who later defected to the United States, the young Romanian first came to international prominence at the 1975 European Championships where she won three gold medals and one silver beating her idol, the Soviet star Lyudmilla Turisheva.

Initially the media attention in the gymnastic halls of the Montreal Games was focussed squarely upon the Soviet trio of Turisheva, Olga Korbut and Nelli Kim. Korbut had just been awarded an outstanding 9.90 in the asymmetric bars when the little Romanian began her routine. There followed a display of exquisite grace and timing after which an anxious Comăneci stared at the electronic display

awaiting her score. The score flashed up 1.00. After a brief moment of confusion the realisation struck home; Comăneci had become the first gymnast to attain 10.0, the perfect score, in Olympic competition. The Swiss timing hadn't foreseen such a result and couldn't display the correct score!

Comăneci went on to score another six 10.0s during the Montreal Games winning gold medals for individual all-round, balance beam and asymmetric bars, a silver medal in the team all round and a bronze medal in the floor exercise.

ABOVE Nadia Comăneci celebrating in front of the scoreboard which was unable to display the correct score

Combat Sports

OLYMPIC COMPETITION INCLUDES six forms of combat sport; boxing, freestyle wrestling, Greco Roman wrestling, judo, Taekwando and fencing.

First introduced at the 1904 St.Louis Games, boxing remains the only Olympic sport in which professionals are not allowed to compete although many, using the Games as a career stepping stone, have gone on to turn professional with great success including Cassius Clay, brothers Michael and Leon Spinks, Joe Frazier, George Foreman, Lennox Lewis and Wladimir Klitschko. In recent years British success has come in the form of Audley Harrison and Amir Khan.

In Olympic competition boxers fight over three rounds of three minutes in front of a panel of five judges who electronically score the match depending on the number of blows struck with the white panel of the boxer's glove upon the front or sides of his opponent's head or body above the belt. The scoring system itself is not without controversy.

At the Barcelona 1992 Games American Eric Griffin was eliminated from the competition in a second round qualification bout against Spaniard Rafael Lozano. Despite comprehensively outscoring his opponent 19-9, 18-9, 26-17, 8-5, 10-9 in the eyes of the judges, he lost the match 5-6 due to the fact that the judges had not pressed their buttons at the same moments in the action. The resulting uproar caused so much embarrassment to the International Amateur Boxing

Association that they have since restricted all access to the scores of individual judges.

Wrestling takes two forms at the Olympic Games. In freestyle wrestling competitors grapple for two three minute rounds scoring technical points for successfully executed holds, manoeuvres, advantage positions and near-throws. A match may be stopped if a wrestler achieves a fall or a 10 point lead. Greco-Roman wrestling, named in honour of the ancient cultures but actually an invention of nineteenth century France, uses the same basis of scoring as the freestyle competition but wrestlers are not permitted to use their legs for pushing, pressing, squeezing or lifting an opponent. No hold may be taken below the hips.

Judo made its first Olympic appearance as a men's competition at the 1964

BELOW Ivan Fundora of Cuba (in red) and Gennadiy Laliyev of Kazakstan compete during the men's Freestyle wrestling during the Athens 2004 Olympics

Tokyo games. Women's competition was introduced in 1992. Based upon the unarmed elements of various forms of jujitsu it was developed in the 1880s by Dr. Jigoro Kano who, in 1909, was selected as the first Asian member of the International Olympic Committee.

Olympic judo matches last five minutes for male and four minutes for female judoka during which two judges score each competitor on the moves, holds and throws they successfully execute. The best moves are declared Ippon, scoring 10 points and an instant win. Lesser moves are termed Waza-ari, Yuko or Koka. Two Waza-ari in a match counts as Ippon but any other combination only counts as a cumulative score. An unusual but not altogether surprising rule for judokas (judo competitors) to observe is that they must be free of unpleasant body odours and possess short fingernails and toenails.

Taekwando traces its roots back 2000 years to traditional Korean martial arts but was itself only invented in 1957. It first appeared in Olympic competition as a demonstration sport in 1988 and again in 1992 receiving recognition as an Olympic sport for men and for

women at the Sydney Games in 2000. Fights are contested over three rounds of three minutes for male competitors and two minutes for females. Competitors attempt to score points by striking defined target areas on their opponents head and body using the foot below the ankle or the knuckles of the index and middle fingers. All hits below the waist are outlawed.

An Olympic sport since 1896, fencing is one of the few Olympic sports that permitted the participation of professionals prior to the 1980s. A fan of the sport, Baron Pierre de Coubertin himself stated unequivocally that fencing "masters" should be allowed to compete. Women's competitions were introduced to the Olympics at the Paris Games of 1924. Competitions are fought on a 14 metres long 1.8 metres wide piste in three classes based upon the type of weapon used.

The épée is a rigid, heavy blade of triangular cross section with a point covered by a cone and may be used to strike the opponent anywhere on the body. The foil is a very light and flexible weapon with a rectangular profile and a blunt point which may only be used to on the trunk of the body between the collar and the hips. The sabre uses a triangular flexible blade with its point blunted. Both blade and point may be used but contact is only permitted on the body above the waist, the head and the arms. All weapons are electronically wired to accurately record hits, lighting up a lamp as they do so.

BELOW Cuba face Korea in the Men's Team Epee Fencing competition at the 2000 Olympic Games in Sydney

Coubertin

PIERRE DE COUBERTIN WAS BORN on New Years Day, 1863, to rich, aristocratic, devoutly Catholic parents. His father was a religious painter of some note whilst his mother, Marie-Marcelle Gigault de Crisenoy de Mirville was descended from a long line of French noblemen. It was well expected of de Coubertin to follow a nobleman's path in life. Religious orders, law and the military beckoned but despite his strict upbringing de Coubertin was something of a free spirit.

In November 1892, aged just 29, de Coubertin addressed a meeting of the all powerful Union of French Athletic Sports Associations (USFSA) at the Sorbonne, Paris. With the words "let us export our rowers, runners and fencers", de Coubertin reinforced his case for "this grandiose and virtuous work: the re-establishment of the Olympic Games". His audience politely applauded and then turned him down.

Undeterred, de Coubertin persisted with realising his dream and in 1894 called a conference of his own. Invited were representatives from twelve countries whom de Coubertin had selected believing they would be sympathetic to his plans. The conference was a great success and a unanimous vote was taken to revive the Olympic Games with de Coubertin appointed to found an organising committee.

Just four years later, under the direction of Baron Pierre de Coubertin the Games of the First Olympiad were staged.

BELOW A portrait of Pierre de Fredi Baron de Coubertin, the Frenchman who revived the Olympic Games.

Cycling

CYCLE RACING HAS APPEARED AT every Olympics since 1896. There are currently three types of Olympic cycling event: road, track and mountain bike racing. Women's cycle racing was first introduced into Olympic competition in 1988 with professionals of both sexes permitted to compete since 1996.

The road cycling program includes a road race and an individual time trial. The road race begins with a massed start and is contested over a distance between 210 and 240 kilometres on a road based circuit of 12 to 18 kilometres.

In the individual time trail, riders are set off at 60 second intervals to race unaided over a course between 45 and 55 kilometres in length. The winner is the rider who completes the course in the shortest time.

The women's road events take place on the same course as the men's events. However, both events are run over shorter distances: approximately 120 kilometres for the road race and between 25 and 35 kilometres for the individual time trial.

The Olympic track cycling schedule consists of a specialised and varied program of racing.

The 1000 metres match sprint is a tactical game of nerves culminating in a 70kph dash for the line. The time trial is a race against the clock with riders competing individually on the track to record the best time from a standing start for either one kilometre for men or 500 metres for women.

BELOW Bradley Wiggins of Great Britain competes in the men's track cycling individual pursuit during the Athens 2004 Olympic Games

ABOVE Action in the women's mountain bike cross country event during the Athens 2004 Olympic Games

winner is either the first to cross the line or the one who catches the other before the end of the race. The team sprint is similar to the team pursuit but is contest by squads of three riders over just three laps.

The points race, usually 40 kilometres in length, is fast and frantic as riders sprint for points every two kilometres. The race finishes when a rider completes the full distance with victory being awarded to the rider on with the most points that has not been lapped by the first finisher. The Madison is similar to the points race but is contested by teams of two who take turns in riding for points.

1996 heralded the introduction of mountain bike racing into the Olympics. The cross country, held over 40 to 50 kilometres for men and 30 to 40 kilometres for women, is run on dirt tracks and gravel roads with no more than 15 percent of the course crossing tarmac.

BMX racing will debut at the 2008 Beijing as a full Olympic event. It is hoped that this fast moving action will stimulate a young audience and encourage participation by countries not normally considered cycling nations.

In the individual and team pursuits, two riders or teams of four riders compete against each other from a standing start on opposite sides of the track. The

Discontinued Events

WHILST THERE ARE MANY EVENTS that have stood the Olympic test of time there are others that have, for various reasons, not found their way to the modern Games.

The 1900 Paris Games saw Great Britain, actually the touring Devon and Somerset Wanderers XI, take a cricket gold medal after defeating a French team consisting almost entirely of British staff from the Paris embassy, 262 to 104. A nail-biting competition ensued for glory in the Olympic croquet competition resulting in France coming first second and third overall – influenced somewhat by the fact that no other nation participated.

Lacrosse made an interesting appearance at the 1904 St. Louis Games with a Canadian team comprising exclusively of Mohawk Indians including Black Eagle, Red Jacket, Almighty Voice and Man Afraid Soap. The 1908 London Olympics featured motor-boating, the only time a motor powered sport has featured at the Games.

The unusual sport of Pelota Basque, a highly physical ball game played with a bat against a wall, featured at the 1900 Paris Games and has since made reappearances as a demonstration sport at both the 1968 and 1992 Olympics. Jeu de Paume, also known as "real tennis" made a single appearance at the 1908 Games

The 1900 Games included some unusual and dramatic variations of equestrian sports including the high jump,

long jump and four-in-hand mail coach. In 1920 figure riding was added to the program. Open to army officers only, this event included jumping on and off and standing upon a horse and even jumping over horses.

Fighting broke out at the 1924 Games as 40,000 passionate French fams looked on in dismay as their team was defeated 17-3 by the unfavoured United States in the last Olympic rugby match to be held. Daniel Carroll made history winning a gold medal as part of the American side at the 1920 Antwerp Games having won an Olympic gold medal twelve years earlier as a member of the conquering Australian team.

Tug of war was a popular event until its discontinuation after the 1920 Antwerp Games. After being pulled over in the first round of the 1908 Games by Great Britain, a protest was lodged by the American team that their opponents were wearing illegal boots. The protest was disallowed after it was pointed out that the team consisted of members of the Liverpool Police and that they were wearing standard issue police boots.

Dityatin

RUSSIAN GYMNAST ALEKSANDR Dityatin achieved a notable first whilst competing at the 1980 Moscow Olympics. Previously, at the 1976 Montreal Games, Dityatin had won silver medals on the rings and as part of the Soviet team narrowly missing out on the individual all-round bronze medal by 0.05 points. Performing on home soil at the Moscow Games Dityatin was determined to improve on his 1976 results.

At every Olympics since 1956 Japan had won the team event, relegating the Soviets to second place. In front of a jubilant Muscovite crowd Dityatin and the Soviet team reversed the 24 year drought by taking the gold medal. The fact that Japan had boycotted the Moscow Games may have been influential! At the end of the team competition the six male finalists for each of the six individual events were named. Dityatin had qualified for them all.

There followed the most extraordinary performance as Dityatin, competing in six finals, won six medals: a gold medal on the rings, silver medals for the

horizontal bar, parallel bars, long horse vault and pommel horse and a bronze for his floor exercise. With his vault, Dityatin had become the first male gymnast to be awarded a 10.0 in Olympic competition. The combined results were good enough to earn him another gold medal as winner of the individual all-round.

Dityatin's greatest achievement of the 1980 Games is that he became the first and only athlete in Olympic history to win eight medals at one Olympiad.

ABOVE Aleksandr Dityatin poses after winning the gold medal in the men's all-around individual competition at the Olympic Games in Moscow 1980

Dream Team

WHEN, IN APRIL 1989, THE International Amateur Basketball Federation (F.I.B.A.) voted 56 to 14 in favour of allowing professional players to compete at the Olympics it heralded a new beginning in the sport. Rumours circulated that the United States had engineered the vote following its semi-final defeat to the Soviet Union in 1988 but they were in fact one of the thirteen nations who voted against the change fearful that the presence of its well paid basketball stars would create a one sided competition. On the other hand, many of the eastern basketball nations were enthusiastic about the ruling as it would allow their players to gain experience in the NBA whilst remaining eligible for Olympic competition.

And so the Dream Team was formed. Coached by the great Chuck Daly and captained by legends Larry Bird and Magic Johnson, the United States team that attended the 1992 Barcelona Olympics was arguably the greatest collection of basketball talent ever assembled. With a roster including Michael Jordan, Charles Barclay and Patrick Ewing the Dream Team scored in excess of 100 points in every game, averaging an astonishing 117.25 points, going forward to defeat Croatia 117 to 85 in the final.

Drugs

THERE ARE FEW SPORTING COMPE-
titions that have not at some point been
tainted by the use of performance
enhancing drugs. The Olympic Games is
no exception, even in its formative years.

During the marathon event at the
1900 St. Louis Olympics, a suffering
Thomas Hicks of the United States was
administered a cocktail of strychnine
and brandy by his helpers. Hicks strug-
gled on to finish and take the gold
medal but had lost almost 5 kilograms
in body weight during the three and a
half hours spent running.

Matters came to a head during the
road race at the 1960 Rome Games when
Danish cyclist Knut Jensen collapsed and
died after consuming a combination of
amphetamines and nicotinyl tartrate.

It may be surprising to learn that
control over the use of performance
enhancing substances was only introduced by the Medical Commission of
the International Olympic Committee
in 1967. Unfortunate Swedish pentath-
lete Hans-Gunnar Liljenwall became
the first athlete to fall foul of the new
regulations during the Mexico City

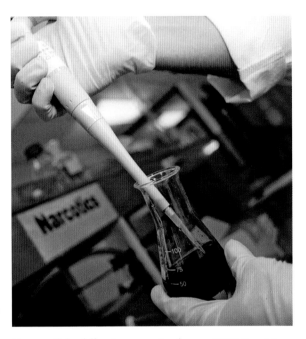

Games of the following year. Anxious
prior to the shooting phase of the competition he had drunk two beers to
calm his nerves and subsequently
tested positive for alcohol.

Mandatory drug testing was introduced at the 1972 Munich Olympics but
already the doctors and coaches
involved in administering performance

ABOVE General view
of urine testing at the
Australian Government
Analytical Laboratories
Olympic Drug Testing
Facilities

ABOVE Ben Johnson crosses the finish line to win the Olympic 100 metre final in a world record 9.79 at the 1988 Olympics. Johnson was later disqualified for failing to pass a drug test

Olympic team between 1968 and 1989. The German authorities, convinced that the Olympics were a great weapon of Cold War propaganda, started experimenting with the use of steroids and testosterone. Despite its banned status, by 1978 East German athletes in all sports were being administered anabolic steroids, in many cases without their own knowledge.

For many years positive tests in Olympic competition were, in the main, given by weightlifters and athletes of a lesser public profile. This changed at the 1988 Seoul Games when Canadian 100 metres winner Ben Johnson was stripped of his gold medal and world record after testing positive for stanozolol. For the first time it was a major athlete and a hero of the games who had been caught cheating.

Drugs continue to be an issue in Olympic sport with substances being added to the banned list on a regular basis. Unfortunately with the pressures on athletes to perform and the huge sums of money now involved in professional sponsorship deals it seems inevitable that unscrupulous doctors and trainers will always strive to stay one step ahead of the testing authorities.

enhancing drugs were ahead of the Medial Commission. New substances were formulated and masking agents were developed that tests were unable to detect.

An incredible example of doping en masse existed within the East German

Equestrian

THE FIRST APPEARANCE OF AN equestrian event on a modern Olympic programme took place at the Paris Games of 1900 in the form of a show-jumping competition. The 1900 Games also included equestrian high and long jumps and a mail coach driving competition. Three equestrian sports are contested at the Games for both individual and team medals: show jumping, dressage and the three-day event.

In the show jumping competition, each horse and rider is required to complete two rounds over a course. The first course of approximately 700 metres in length comprises 12 to 15 jumps varying between 1.4 metres and 1.6 metres in height and must include a water obstacle. The second course of 10 jumps must differ from the first and be no longer than 600 metres. Points, known as faults, are awarded should a

horse refuse a jump or knock over a pole on a fence. Additional points are awarded if either the horse or its rider fall or if the time limit for the course is exceeded. The winner is the rider/horse combination with the least number of faults. Should there be a tie for first place then a jump-off using several elements of the second course decides the outcome.

The objective of dressage is to express the responsiveness of a horse to its rider's commands. A series of complex, pre-defined manoeuvres in all equine paces – walk, trot and canter - are performed in the presence of a panel of judges. Horse and rider and marked on how well they perform each manoeuvre, the regularity of the paces, the impulsion of the horse, the submis-

ABOVE German dressage rider Ulla Salzgeber rides on her horse at Markopoulo Olympic Equestrian Centre during the final of the individual dressage competition in Athens, 2004

ABOVE Jeanette Brakewell of Great Britain competes in the eventing cross country competition during the Athens 2004 Olympic Games

RIGHT An obstacle in the individual three day eventing jumping final competition during the Athens 2004 Olympic Games

siveness of the horse and the form and position of the rider. In Olympic competition the top third of the field after an initial test go forward to a second round from which the best 15 riders advance to the final, a freestyle round performed to music.

The three-day event combines the disciplines of dressage and show jumping with each horse also required to complete a gruelling cross country course. The sport of eventing was originally derived from the exercises devised to test the suitability of horses for the military. Until recently the cross country phase was part of a wider ranging endurance section in which competitors were required to also perform two road-and-tracks courses and a steeplechase but these have now been dropped in favour of the preferred short-course format.

Ewry

American Ray Ewry must be considered one of the greatest Olympians of all time but his legend remains almost unknown because the three events at which he excelled are no longer part of the Games.

Born in Lafayette, Indiana in 1873, Ewry spent much of his youth confined to a wheelchair having contracted polio. Determined to beat his affliction, the young Ewry started to exercise. As his confidence grew so did his strength. Perseverance paid dividends as Ewry not only regained the use of both of his legs but developed into an outstanding athlete specialising in standing jumps.

Competing at the 1900 Paris Olympics, Ewry gained notoriety as "the human frog" by winning gold medals for the standing high jump, standing long jump, at which he set a new world record, and the standing triple jump.

Another Olympics, another moniker. Dubbed "the rubber man" by the American public, Ewry repeated his three-way

clean sweep at the 1904 St. Louis Games, this time taking the world record for the standing long jump with a distance of 3.47 metres.

With the standing triple jump eliminated from Olympic competition, Ewry was only able to enter two events at the 1908 London Olympics. Predictably he won both adding another two gold medals to his tally.

Ewrys story is not only remarkable considering his recovery from polio but also because he is the only athlete in Olympic history to have won eight gold medals.

BELOW Ray Ewry of the USA in action during the Standing High Jump event at the 1908 London Olympics, for which he won the gold medal

Flo-Jo

TWENTY-NINE YEAR OLD Los Angeles born Florence Griffith burst on the Olympic scene at the 1984 Games. Despite a creditable silver medal in the women's 200 metres, media and public attention of Griffith was directed at her outrageously long, painted finger nails rather than her athletic ability.

Following the games, athletics took a back seat in Griffith's life. Marrying 1984 Olympic triple jump champion Al Joyner, she worked in a bank then as a beautician. Returning to competition prior to the 1988 Seoul Games, 200 metre specialist Florence Griffith-Joyner amazed Olympic selectors by running the 100 metres in 10.49 seconds, a new world record.

Dubbed Flo-Jo by the public, Griffith-Joyner soon became one of the stars of Seoul. Easily winning the women's 100 metres, Flo-Jo went on to win a gold medal in the 200 metres, setting an unbroken world record of 21.34 seconds, a gold medal in the 4x100 metres relay and a silver medal in the 4x400 metres relay, the first time she had competed over the distance.

The athlete who had returned was very different from the one who had competed at the 1984 Games. Her stature was that of a body-builder, her jaw-line had squared and her voice had deepened. Although Flo-Jo never once tested positive for drugs, the fact that she retired the day before the introduction of mandatory random drug testing fuelled speculation.

In September 1998 Florence Griffith-Joyner died in her sleep aged 39.

Fraser

AUSTRALIAN DAWN FRASER WAS taught to swim at the age of five by her brother Donald. A natural in the water, Fraser began competing at the age of eleven and was spotted by coach Harry Gallagher at the age of twelve.

Fraser's first taste of international competition was the 1956 Melbourne Olympics. Competing in the 100 metres freestyle final she and compatriot Lorraine Crapp pulled away from the field with Fraser taking the gold medal and setting a new world record. Success continued with a gold medal in the 4x100 metres freestyle relay and a silver medal in the 400 metres freestyle.

Undefeated, Fraser arrived in Rome for the 1960 Games and successfully defended her 100 metres freestyle title. The following day, having stayed up late celebrating, Fraser argued with Australian officials, refusing to swim a heat of the medley relay. Despite these problems, Fraser still managed to win two more silver medals in the 4x100 metres freestyle and medley relays.

Disaster struck during preparation for the 1964 Tokyo Olympics when her car crashed into a truck killing her mother and leaving Fraser in a neck brace. Remarkably Fraser recovered in time for the Games where, undeterred, she successfully defended her 100 metres freestyle crown and took silver in the 4x100 metres freestyle relay.

Fraser's career ended after being arrested for shinning up a flagpole at Emperor Hirohito's Palace to collect a souvenir. The charges were dropped and Hirohito gave Fraser the flag as a present but these antics were too much for the Australian Swimming Union who issued a ten year ban for her indiscretion.

BELOW Australian swimming Champion Dawn Fraser (C-without cap) dives for victory in the Olympic ladies 100m free style in October 1964 in Tokyo

Gabrselassie

RIGHT Haile Gebrselassie of Ethiopia speeds over the track to win the Olympic men's 10,000m gold medal in the Sydney Olympic Games, 2000

MANY ATHLETES HAVE WON MORE medals than Haile Gabrselassie but few have provided such exciting races. One of 10 children, Gabrselassie was born on a farm outside the Ethiopian village of Assela from which, every day, he ran the 20 kilometres to school and back with his books tucked under his arm.

Gabrselassie arrived at the 1996 Atlanta Games as favourite for the 10,000 metres title although competition was expected from Kenyan Paul Tergat. In the final Tergat pulled away after 8,000 metres, closely stalked by the Ethiopian. With one lap to go Gabrselassie pulled alongside and looked at his rival then sprinted away to win the gold medal.

As the world record holder and undefeated in a 10,000 metres final in seven years, many expected Gabrselassie to be favourite for the 2000 Sydney Olympics. However, his preparation was disrupted due to a tendon injury. In a race always regarded as one of the greatest in Olympic history, Gabrselassie spent time closely tracking the leader and controlling the pace. With seven laps remaining Kenyan John Korir attacked reducing the field to seven contenders including Gabrselassie and his rival Tergat. Boxed in with only one lap to go, Tergat pounced at the 250 metres mark. Gabrselassie fought back, pulling alongside the Kenyan with just 50 metres to go. The two battled side by side to the line where Gabrselassie dipped forward to take victory by 0.09 seconds.

Returning to the Olympics in 2004 with the intention of becoming the first man in history to win three consecutive gold medals in the 10,000 metres Gabrselassie, hampered by a tendon injury, could only achieve fifth behind compatriot Kenenisa Bekele.

Gymnastics

GYMNASTICS WERE FIRST SEEN AT the Olympics during the inaugural Games of 1896 at which time the events contested included rope-climbing and club swinging. Women gymnastics were introduced as a team event in 1928 with individual competition not being established until the Helsinki Games of 1952. Competition is split into artistic and rhythmic disciplines.

The artistic events comprise three stages – a team competition, an individual all-round competition and individual apparatus finals. A gymnast from a nation unable to send a full team must still compete in the team competition as it is used as individual qualification. Each nation enters a team of six gymnasts who perform on each of the apparatus – horizontal bar, parallel bars, long horse vault, pommel horse, rings and floor in the case of male competitors and vault, asymmetric bars, balance beam and floor for females. Following a qualification round the best eight teams progress to the team final. Two judges asses the difficulty of the routine whilst a further six judges mark every com-

petitor out of ten for each exercise. The highest and lowest mark is discarded with the remaining two averaged to give the score. The team event is scored by taking the best of a nation's results across all the apparatus and adding them together to give a team total.

BELOW Russian gymnast Alina Kavaeva performs with a rope during the women's individual all-around final for Rhythmic Gymnastics

The 36 highest scoring individual gymnasts from the team competition advance to an individual all-round final although a maximum of three from each nation is permitted. From this competition, the eight highest performing competitors on each apparatus progress to the individual apparatus finals although only two gymnasts per nation may compete on any given apparatus.

Trampoline was added to the Olympic programme at the 2000 Games in Sydney with competitions for men and for women. A qualification event comprising compulsory and optional routines is followed by a final contested by the top eight competitors. In this they are required to perform 10 optional moves judged for difficulty and execution.

The rhythmic gymnastics were introduced into the Olympics Games for the first time in 1984 and takes the form of an all-round competition. Competitors perform a musically accompanied freestyle routine in a 12 metres square area using each of four apparatus which are chosen for each Olympic competition from five available options – hoop, ribbon, ball, rope and club. These apparatus may be in any colour with the exception of gold, silver and bronze. A gymnast's routine is judged for composition and execution by a panel of judges.

Helsinki 1952

FOR THE ORGANISERS AT LEAST, the 1952 Helsinki Olympic Games were to pose a number of difficult questions. Eastern Bloc participation was considered essential in maintaining an international spirit but the host nation had suffered terribly following the Soviet invasion of 1939. Despite this a strong Soviet team did attend taking a total of 71 medals, 22 of them gold. Russian Aleksandra Chudina showed her versatility by winning silver medals in the long jump and javelin and a bronze medal in the high jump.

Germany, banned from the 1948 Olympics but no longer considered an aggressor, returned to the Games. However, having become a divided nation only athletes from the Federal Republic would compete. Japan also made their first appearance since the 1936 Games.

Having previously won a 10,000 metres gold and silver in the 5,000 metres at the 1948 London Olympics, Czechoslovakian long distance runner Emile Zátopek, through a series of outstanding achievements, stole the 1952 Games. Four days after successfully defending his 10,000 metre title, he would take the 5,000 metres gold that had eluded him four years previously. Later that week Zátopek sprinted home to victory in the marathon winning by an incredible 2 minute margin. It was the first time he had ever competed in a marathon in his life!

BELOW Finnish runner Nurmi, a former gold medalist, lighting the Olympic flame at the opening ceremonies for the Olympics in Helsinki

How Many?

AS THE OLYMPIC GAMES MOVE well into the twenty-first century their significance and size has grown almost beyond recognition.

The inaugural Athens Games of 1896 were a small affair when compared to the leviathan that is the modern Olympics. With only nine sports on the program – track and field, cycling, fencing, gymnastics, wrestling, weightlifting, shooting, swimming and tennis - just 43 medal events were contested by a total of 245 athletes, all of whom were male, in the presence of an estimated 80,000 spectators. Of the 14 nations represented all were from Europe with the exception of the United States, Chile and Egypt.

Returning 108 years later to its spiritual home of Athens for the 2004 Games, the Olympic experience had grown almost beyond comparison. Medals were contested in 301 events over 28 sports which now included triathlon, beach volleyball and Taekwando. An astounding 202 nations were represented by 11,099 athletes, 4,517 of whom were women, from countries as far a field as Burkina Faso and Kiribati. The games were administered by 5,500 accredited officials and kept secure by 45,000 security personnel whilst 16,000 broadcasting engineers, cameramen and presenters kept a global audience of 4.5 billion viewers informed and 5,500 journalists kept the back pages of the newspapers full.

BELOW A statue promoting Beijing''s bid to host the 2008 Olympic Games

IOC

THE INTERNATIONAL Olympic Committee (IOC) was formed by Baron Pierre de Coubertin on 23 June 1894 with the task of reinstating the Olympic Games in a modern form. The IOC has continued its work and is now responsible for the administration of all Olympic related matters under the watchful eye of its president, Jacques Rogge.

The 115 members of the committee itself were originally co-opted, with royalty and members of the aristocracy being favoured. However, in recent years there has been an important drive towards the allocation of seats to athletes and leaders of international and national federations in an attempt to better represent the world of sport.

Every four years an executive board of the IOC will choose five locations as candidate cities from a list of applicants based upon their responses to a standard questionnaire. The committee members are then responsible for voting on which city is to be awarded the summer and winter Olympics.

The IOC has in recent years been implicated in a number of scandals involving unscrupulous committee members taking advantage of their position to gain favours from candidate cities but has now taken action to clean up its tarnished image.

ABOVE Members of the International Olympic Committee during the 1896 Olympic Games in Athens, Greece.

Johnson

MICHAEL JOHNSON IS ONE OF THE greatest athletes ever to grace an Olympic Games. His unique, head bobbing upright running style earned him the nickname "The Duck". When asked "If you had a usual running technique like other runners do you think you would go faster?" he responded "If I ran like all the other runners, I would be back there with them".

Johnson's first Olympic appearance was Barcelona 1992. Ranked world number one, the Texan was expected to take the 200 metres title but, twelve days before the start of the Games, Johnson contracted food poisoning whilst at a restaurant. Weakened, he was eliminated in the semi-finals allowing compatriot Michael Marsh to take the gold. As consolation Johnson collected a gold medal as part of the victorious U.S. 4x400 metres relay team.

In Atlanta Johnson made amends. Competing in gold running shoes, he easily won the 400 metres final by over a second from Britain's Roger Black then in the 200 metres final he made history. Recovering after a poor start, Johnson powered through the bend until with 90 metres to go he went into light-speed to win by four metres, demolishing his own world record by 0.34 seconds, having run the last 100 metres in 9.20 seconds.

Missing out on 200 metres selection due to injury, Johnson headed to the Sydney with the 400 metres in his sights once more. In the final he was again the slowest to start but with 100 metres remaining he pulled away to win by four metres becoming the first man to win twice at the distance. To finish a perfect career Johnson again won a gold medal in the 4x400 metres relay.

Kayaks and Canoes

CANOEING HAS BEEN PART OF THE Olympics since the Berlin Games of 1936 with events for women being included from 1948. The canoeing events are split into two types – kayaks and Canadians.

Kayaks, which are derived from the craft of the Inuit tribes, have a pointed bow and stern and a closed in deck. The competitor sits within the craft with their legs stretched forward using a long double ended paddle to propel themselves forward. In flat-water races the kayak makes use of a small rudder to trim its course.

Canadian canoes, developed from those of the native North Americans, bring the competitor into a kneeling position and feature either an open deck for flat-water races or a closed deck for slaloms. The paddle used in this type is shorter and single bladed being switched from side to side to control and propel the canoe.

Separate flat-water competitions are held for both kayaks and Canadians over 500 and 1000 metres and are contested by individuals and pairs. A 1000 metres flat-water event is also held for team of four using special kayaks over 11 metres long.

Slalom events require the competitor to paddle down a fast flowing course whilst negotiating their way through 25 gates, six of which must be upstream. If the competitor touches a gate they incur penalty points, the winner being the canoeist with the best combined time and penalty score.

BELOW Miss Richards an 1948 Olympic contender.

Korbut

GYMNAST OLGA KORBUT WAS BORN in the Belarusian city of Grodno in 1955. Known as the Sparrow of Minsk she took up gymnastics at the age of eight, entering a training school aged 11 years under the guidance Renald Knysh.

Competing at her first Olympic Games in 1972, the tiny 17 year old cap-

tured the hearts of the Munich crowds and wowed a television audience with an outstanding asymmetric bar performance in the team event. Finishing third athlete overall in the team competition, Korbut appeared capable of causing an upset in the individual competition.

Two days later the individual all-round final started. To the delight of the crowds and media Korbut moved into the lead at the halfway point. The asymmetric bars upon which she had performed so well in the team competition were next. Disaster struck. Mounting the bars she scuffed the mat then during the routine she fell from the bars and missed a simple manoeuvre. Unable to hide her disappointment she returned to the bench and wept as the judges awarded her a lowly 7.50.

The next day, in the individual apparatus finals, her form returned. With the world watching on television, she won a silver medal on the asymmetric bars and then gold medals for the balance beam and the floor exercise.

Korbut's subsequent fame was such that back home in Grodno the local post office had to employ a special clerk to sort the 20,000 fan letters she received each year.

Latynina

THE GYMNAST LARISA LATYNINA holds the record for the most outstanding overall achievement by an Olympic athlete. Growing up in the Ukrainian town of Kherson she took to ballet at an early age only turning to gymnastics after her instructor moved away. At 19 years old she first competed internationally winning a team gold medal at the 1954 World Championships.

Her Olympic debut came at the 1956 Melbourne Games. The young Latynina fought hard against the more experienced Hungarian Agnes Keleti to take gold medals in the individual and team all-round competitions. To this she added gold medals on the floor and vault, a silver medal on the asymmetric bars and a bronze medal in the now discontinued portable apparatus event.

Latynina arrived in Rome for the 1960 Games as the clear favourite. Winning the individual all-round competition for a second time she then led the Soviets to a decisive win in the team competition. Successfully defending her floor title, she then took silver medals for the balance beam and asymmetric bars and a bronze medal in the vault.

Returning for her third Games at the 1964 Tokyo Olympics, Latynina won gold medals in the floor event and for the all-round team but was finally defeated in the all-round competition by Czech Vera Cáslavská securing only a silver medal. A silver medal in the vault and bronze medals for the asymmetric bars and balance beam added to her overall Olympic medal tally.

Larissa Latynina finished her Olympic career the holder of eighteen Olympic medals; nine gold medals, five silver and four bronze and remains to this day the Games' most prolific medal winner.

ABOVE Larissa Latynina performs her routine on the beam during the Olympic Games in Melbourne, 1956

Lewis

RIGHT Carl Lewis in action in the finals of the Men's Olympic long jump competition, Barcelona, 1992

BELOW Carl Lewis proudly carries the American flag after winning the 100 metres at the Olympic Games in Los Angeles

BORN IN BIRMINGHAM, ALABAMA, in the summer of 1961 the son of two athletics coaches, Lewis grew up in New Jersey taking to athletics as a teenager. His first Olympic selection was short lived with the United States team boycotting the Moscow Games of 1980. Lewis had wait for the Los Angeles Olympics in 1984 to make an impact.

Having achieved victory in the 100 metres, long jump and 4x100 metres at the 1983 World Championships Lewis was considered a favourite for success in Los Angeles. His goal was to emulate his hero, Jesse Owens, by winning all three plus the 200 metres. This he did with ease setting new world 4x100 metres and Olympic 200 metres records in the process.

Hoping to repeat this performance at the 1998 Seoul Games, he won the 100 metres following the disqualification of Canadian Ben Johnson but suffered a surprise defeat in the 200 metres by fellow countryman Joe DeLoach. The US 4x100 metres team was then disqualified in the heats. As a consolation he easily defended his long jump title.

Defending his long jump crown at the 1992 Barcelona Games Lewis found himself pushed close by compatriot Michael Powell. Despite this he retained his title by a narrow margin to win his third Olympic long jump title. Running the anchor leg of the 4x100 metres Lewis secured another gold medal and yet another world record.

Returning to the Olympics in Atlanta he was not expected to make an impact having barely qualified at the US Olympic trials. Proving the doubters wrong Lewis put in a massive 8.50 metres leap to secure his ninth Olympic gold medal. An achievement shared by only three other athletes.

London 1908

FOLLOWING THE APRIL 1906 ERUPtion of Mount Vesuvius the Italian government, considering its resources best placed elsewhere, requested the planned 1908 Rome Olympics be moved. The IOC obliged, relocating the games to London. A new stadium with running track, swimming pool, cycling track and a football pitch was hastily constructed in Shepherd's Bush.

At the opening ceremony, in the presence of King Edward VII, athletes marched into the stadium in national teams behind their national flag for the first time, a tradition upheld ever since.

Willy & Lottie Dod, representing Great Britain, became the first brother and sister medallists respectively collecting gold and silver in the archery. Swede Oscar Swahn became the Olympic Games oldest gold medallist, out-shooting 14 rivals to win the single-shot running deer competition. America's Ray Ewry won the standing high jump and standing long jump competitions for the third time becoming the only person to win a career total of eight individual Olympic gold medals.

Italian Dorando Pietri captured the hearts of the public in a dramatic finale to the marathon. On entering the stadium after 26 miles Pietri collapsed five times before being helped across the finishing line by officials subsequently being disqualified for receiving external assistance.

BELOW The start of the Marathon at Windsor Castle which finished at the Olympic stadium in Shepherds Bush, London. 1908

London 1948

THE 1940 GAMES, AWARDED TO Tokyo, were hastily reallocated to Helsinki following Japan's invasion of China, but the winds of change were blowing over a much wider area. The subsequent Soviet invasion of Finland and the encroaching prospect of a war in Europe saw the 1940 Games and the planned 1944 London Olympics cancelled all together.

The task of organising the first postwar Olympic Games was never going to be an easy one but, with typical resolve, it was the British Olympic Committee that would step in to fill the breech. There would be three notable absences from the 1948 Games. Germany, who were banned from competition and not invited, Japan who although invited declined to attend and the Soviet Union who were in a state of sporting and political isolation. Incredibly 59 nations were still represented with over 4,000 athletes taking part.

In many cases facilities would be Spartan – athletes were accommodated in army barracks – but there would be a taste of the Games to come as, for the first time, television cameras were present with events being broadcast to an expectant nation.

Czechoslovakian canoeist Jan Brzák and Hungarian fencer Ilona Elek surprised many by both retaining the respective titles they had won at the 1936 Berlin Olympics. At one point in the competition Elek had trailed American Maria Cerra 2-0, but a remarkable four successive hits took her through to a final bout against Denmark's Karen Lachmann which she won 4-2 to take the Gold.

BELOW British athlete John Mark lights the Olympic Flame at the opening ceremony

The undoubted star of the Games was 30 year old Fanny Blankers-Koen of Holland. A world record holder in six disciplines, Blankers-Koen was restricted by an Olympic regulation that permitted an athlete to enter only four events. Choosing to compete in the 100m, 200m, 80m hurdles and the 4x100m relay she proved her dominance returning home with four gold medals.

Audrey Patterson of the United States made Olympic history by taking third place behind Blankers-Koen in the 200m becoming the first black female athlete to win an Olympic medal. Compatriot Alice Coachman would, the next day, take victory in the high jump to become the first black female gold medallist.

Perhaps the most amazing achievement of the Games was that of Hungarian pistol shooter Karoly Takács. A member of the 1938 World Championship winning team, Takács had lost his shooting hand to a grenade during the war. Undeterred, he taught himself to shoot left-handed and in doing so earned himself an Olympic Gold medal in the rapid-fire pistol shoot.

ABOVE A BBC camera films the proceedings at Wembley Stadium as King George VI takes the March Past 6,000 athletes representing 58 countries, at the Opening Ceremony of the 1948 London Olympics

MIDDLE Richard Burnell and Bertram Bushnell of Great Britain near the finish at Henley-on-Thames, soon to become the winners in the Double Sculls Final

Los Angeles 1932

RIGHT Mildred Didrikson of the USA throws the javelin to win the gold medal

THE GREAT DEPRESSION WOULD take its toll even upon the Olympics. With millions unemployed worldwide following the 1929 Wall Street crash and the sinister rise of extremist attitudes in parts of Europe a mere 1,503 athletes attended the Los Angeles Games of 1932.

Despite these difficulties the Games were far from a failure. Record crowds, including many Hollywood celebrities, flocked to the games; the Opening Ceremony at the L.A. Coliseum attracted 100,000 spectators. Incredibly, considering the incumbent economic climate, the 1932 Olympics were the first Games to turn a profit.

It would be another Olympic of firsts. The three tiered victory rostrum was introduced as was the protocol of raising the national flag of a victorious competitor. Electronic timing and photo-finishes were included officially (having made their unofficial debut at the 1912 Games) and for the first time a medal result was changed after a photo finish review. A true sportsman American Jack Keller, who had incorrectly been awarded a bronze medal in the 110m hurdles tracked down Briton Donald Finley to personally hand over his medal.

Despite qualifying for five track and field events, Olympic rules prevented American Mildred Didrikson from competing in more than three. World records in the high jump and 80m hurdles and victory in the javelin have assured her a place in Olympic history.

Los Angeles 1984

LOS ANGELES WAS THE ONLY CITY prepared to bid for the right to host the 1984 Games, other nations having been deterred by the terrorist actions of the Munich Games and the financial debacle of those in Montreal. For the first time since 1896, the Games became dependent on the financial support of corporate sponsorship as significant federal funding was not made available. Unwittingly these games would set the blueprint for future Olympics.

Unsurprisingly, considering the US led boycott of the Moscow Games, the Soviet Union declined their invitation to attend citing anti-communist demonstrations in the USA and a worry for the safety of their athletes as the reason. Compared to the 65 nations that had rejected their invitations to the 1980 Olympics, only 14 declined to attend the 1984 Games in support of the USSR. This number may seem small but these nations accounted for 58% of the gold medals awarded at the 1976 Montreal Games. In total a record 140 nations

were represented at the 1984 Olympics.

In winning gold medals in the men's 100m, 200m, long jump and the 4x100m relay 23 year old American Carl Lewis not only delighted the thoroughly partisan crowd but also matched the 1936 achievement of his hero, Jesse Owens. 1976 400m hurdles gold medallist Edwin Moses won the event for the second time having missed out in 1980 due to the western boycott.

The Los Angeles games would see a number of Olympic firsts for female

ABOVE Joan Benoit does a victory lap carrying a US flag after winning the women's marathon

ABOVE View of the human Olympic ring formations

RIGHT The women's 3,000 metre race with left to right Wendy Sly of Great Britain (silver medal), Zola Budd of Great Britain (gold medal), Maricica Puica of Romania and Mary Decker of the USA

athletes. American Joan Benoit won the first women's marathon with her compatriot, Connie Carpenter-Phinney, winning the inaugural women's cycling road race. Other events to be added included women's rhythmic gymnastics and synchronised swimming.

Controversy surrounded the final of the women's 3000m as barefoot British athlete Zola Budd collided with favourite Mary Decker of the USA, bringing her to the ground. Although it was apparent that Decker was largely at fault it was Budd who would feel the wrath of the nationalist American public.

German Ulrike Meyfarth had set a record at the 1972 Games in winning the high jump and becoming the youngest winner of an individual track and field event. In 1984 she again won that title becoming the oldest ever winner of the event.

In the rowing a young and little known Steve Redgrave representing Great Britain won his first Olympic gold medal giving spectators a tast of what was to come over the next 16 years.

Louganis

OF SWEDISH / SAMOAN DESCENT, Greg Louganis was adopted by a Greek-American family having been given up by his fifteen year old parents. Constantly bullied by his classmates due to his dyslexia and dark skin, by the age of nine Louganis was smoking tobacco and by twelve he had moved on to marijuana becoming dependent on alcohol as a teenager. He found his escape in diving.

Qualifying for the 1976 Montreal Olympics at the age of sixteen he won a silver medal in the platform dive and finished a respectable sixth in the springboard. Unfortunately due to the American boycott of the Moscow Games it was 1984 before he could re-enter the Olympic arena.

Ignoring the pressure of being favourite, Louganis executed a series of outstanding dives, first winning the springboard with an unprecedented 92 points then executing a perfect reverse tuck to take the platform becoming the first diver to score in excess of 700 points in the event and the first since 1928 to win both medals.

Returning to the Games in 1988, Louganis miscalculated his ninth dive in the springboard preliminaries cracking the back of his head on the board. With sutures applied he dived once more attaining the highest score of the day going on to take the gold medal in the final. The platform competition was much closer than in 1994. Only by performing a difficult reverse 3_ somersault in tuck was Louganis able to take gold by the narrowest of margins from 14 year old Xiong Ni of China.

BELOW Greg Louganis bangs his head against the board after mistiming his dive during the Olympic competition in Seoul

Mascots

SINCE THEIR INTRODUCTION AT the 1972 Munich Games the Olympic mascot has become an integral part of the Olympic image. Its purpose is to promote the culture and history of the host city and to convey the spirit of the Games, especially to younger generations.

Waldi, a brightly coloured dachshund, had the honour of being the first Olympic mascot. An instant hit with the public, his qualities of resistance, tenacity and agility were said to mirror those require in an Olympic athlete.

Amik the Beaver was introduced for the 1976 Montreal Games. The name Amik, meaning beaver, was taken from the Algonquian language of the Native Americans. The beaver was chosen to represent hard work.

Created by a famous Russian illustrator of children's books, Victor Chizikov, Misha the Bear, mascot for the 1980

ABOVE The Athens 2004 summer games official mascots Phevos (L) and Athena

RIGHT Giant inflatable mascots for the Beijing Olympics in 2008

Moscow Games, remains the most popular and instantly recognisable Olympic mascot of all time.

Not to be outdone by their Eastern adversaries, American organisers enlisted Walt Disney to design Sam the Eagle, mascot of the 1984 Los Angeles Olympics. Resplendent in full star-spangled garb, Sam was the first mascot to be thoroughly exploited for commercial purposes somewhat echoing the feel of the 1984 Games themselves.

Sporting a traditional Korean hat with the Olympic rings suspended from a ribbon around his neck, Hodori the

Tiger was designed by Kim Hyun as the mascot for the 1988 Seoul Olympics. A friendly character, Hodori reflects the hospitable nature of the Korean people. His name is derived from the Korean words Ho, meaning tiger, and Dori, a jovial term for little boys.

Cobi the Dog, created by Valencian artist Javier Mariscal, with his smart shirt and tie and beaming smile was chosen as the mascot of the 1992 Barcelona Games. Cobi starred in his own series on Spanish television preceding the Olympics.

The first mascot to be designed using computers was Izzy for the 1996 Atlanta Games. Like a being from a video game, this confused character's name was created because nobody seemed to quite know what it was.

Olly, Syd and Millie, their names derived from the words Olympic, Sydney and Millennium, were the first multiple mascots for an Olympic Games. Representing generosity, environment and technology these characters heralded a new chapter in Olympic history.

Based upon ancient dolls found in Greece, brother and sister Phevos and Athena were the mascots of the 2004 Athens Games and are named after the Greek god of light and music and the goddess of wisdom.

For the 2008 Beijing Olympics the Chinese organisers have created five mascots. Known collectively as The Friendlies, each has a rhyming two syllable name, used in China as a term of endearment for children. Bèibei the fish is joined by Jīngjing the panda, Huānhuan the Olympic flame, Yingying the Tibetan antelope and Nīni the swallow. When the names are put together they read Běijīng huānyíng nî, which translates as "Beijing Welcomes You".

LEFT Misha the Bear, mascot for the 1980 Moscow Olympics

Medals

RIGHT The commemorative medal from the 1904 St Louis Olympic Games

IT WAS NOT UNTIL THE St. Louis Games of 1904 that gold, silver and bronze medals were awarded for first, second and third place. Prior to this winners would be presented with a silver medal and an olive branch and the runner up a medal on its own. The unfortunate third placed athlete would win nothing more than the congratulations of officials and his peers.

Over the years some athletes have amassed an amazing tally of medals. Ukrainian Gymnast Larissa Latynina boasts the greatest haul winning a stunning eighteen medals, five of which are gold between 1956 and 1964. Russian Nikolai Andrianov holds the overall medal record for men; fifteen overall, seven of which are gold.

The most career Olympic gold medals won by a single competitor are nine. This honour is shared by four athletes: Latynina, Paavo Nurmi of Finland, and Americans Mark Spitz and Carl Lewis. Another gymnast, Vitaly Scherbo of Belarus holds the record for the most gold medals won in a single day having collected four at the 1992 Barcelona Games.

Having won a gold medal at the 1932 Los Angeles Games, Hungarian fencer Aladár Gerevich astonished crowds by repeating the feat at the 1960 Rome Olympics, a gap of 28 years.

Melbourne 1956

WHEN, IN 1949, THE IOC nominated Melbourne as host city to the 1956 Olympic Games they could have not seen the unusual problem that would come to light. It was only in 1954 that the implications of Australia's requirement for all horses to spend a six-month period in quarantine were fully appreciated. With the Games at stake the decision was taken to hold the equestrian events in Stockholm during May – some six months earlier than the events to be held in Melbourne.

Once again the games were surrounded by political intrigue and controversy. Egypt, Iraq and Lebanon withdrew in protest over the occupation by French and British forces of the Suez Canal and the Israeli incursion into Sinai. Switzerland, Spain and the Netherlands absented themselves in reaction to the Soviet invasion of Hungary. China also boycotted the

Games to avoid meeting Taiwan (then known as Formosa). On a more positive note East and West Germany entered a combined team and were warmly received.

Political tensions overflowed as Hungary, the reigning Olympic water polo Champions, were drawn to meet the U.S.S.R. in a match that would decide the outcome of the gold medal. Just a month earlier, on 4 November, 200,000 Soviet troops had quashed the Budapest uprising. Though tactically inferior the Hungarians managed to

ABOVE Australian athlete Ron Clarke carries the Olympic torch into the stadium during the opening ceremony of the 1956 Olympic games in Melbourne

Hungarian Ervin Zádor badly splitting his eyebrow. As blood gushed the fists began to fly, the referee wisely calling the game to a premature halt declaring Hungary the victors.

Ukrainian Viktor Chukarin and Hungary's Ágnes Keleti dominated the gymnastics. Churakin won five medals, three of them gold to bring his lifetime Olympic medal tally to 11 medals whilst Keleti's four gold and two silver medals brought her total to 10.

A new discipline was added to the swimming competition as the butterfly stroke was separated from the breast-stroke with American William Yorzyk taking the gold medal. For the first time the fibreglass pole was used in the pole vault competition (it had previously been used in the 1952 decathlon) assist-ing Georgios Roubanis of Greece to a bronze medal.

With only fifteen minutes to go before the weigh-in, bantamweight weightlifter Charles Vinci of the U.S.A. found himself to be 200 grams over-weight. Only by means of a rather severe military haircut was he able to make the weight and qualify for the competition. Vinci went on to take the gold medal.

stamp their authority on the match playing tight defensive formations and running out exciting and decisive breaks. In the closing minutes Russian Valentin Prokopov struck out at

Mexico City 1968

DUE TO ITS ALTITUDE OF 2,240 metres, the rarefied air of Mexico City contains only 70% of the oxygen found at sea level. The decision to hold the Olympic Games in such conditions was therefore seen as highly controversial. Athletes, coaches and doctors all feared the unknown.

In many cases those fears were justly founded as endurance athletes suffered for their sport. In the 10,000 metres, with six laps to go, two runners were removed on stretchers. With fewer than three laps to go 1500 metre gold medallist Kip Keino of Kenya dropped out suffering from stomach cramps. Victory went to fellow Kenyan Naftali Temu who, in out-sprinting Ethiopian Mamo Wolde, took the gold medal. Australian world record holder Ron Clarke collapsed after finishing in sixth place and was unconscious for over ten minutes.

Whilst the endurance athletes suffered, the "sprint" athletes relished the lofty conditions. World records fell in the men's 100, 200 and 400 metres, the

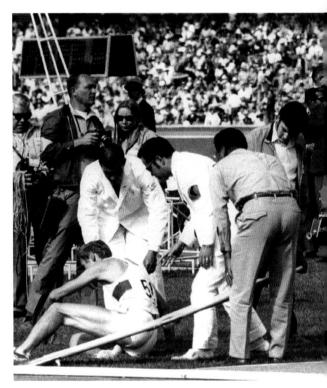

400 meter hurdles, the 4x100m and 4x400m relays, the long jump and the triple jump although there has been speculation as to the validity of some wind readings taken during these

ABOVE Two athletes fall victim to the high altitudes of the 1968 Olympics in Mexico City

ABOVE Balloons being released over the stadium at the opening ceremony of the Olympic Games in Mexico City

City Games of 1968. Two months before the Games Soviet forces had invaded Czechoslovakia forcing gymnast Vera Cáslavská into hiding. After three weeks of concealment Cáslavská emerged to win a remarkable four gold and two silver medals and was then married in front of 10,000 Olympic fans.

Another athlete remembered for his exploits at the 1968 Games is American Dick Fosbury. His revolutionary high jumping technique wowed the excited crowds and baffled his opponents as he went on to take the gold medal with a personal best and Olympic record of 2.24 metres.

Not to be outdone, 22 year old American long jumper Bob Beamon produced an 8.90 metre long jump beating the existing world record by an astounding 55 centimetres. His mark would not be broken for another 22 years.

Sweden has the honour of having fielded what is probably the most unusual team in Olympic history. Their four man silver medal winning squad for the cycling team time trial consisted of Erik Pettersson, Gösta Pettersson, Sture Pettersson and Tomas Pettersson: four brother from the small village of Fåglum.

records. For four of the events the wind was recorded at 2.0 metres per second – the maximum permissible for the ratification of a world record.

One athlete could not fail to win the hearts of all who watched the Mexico

Montreal 1976

THE MONTREAL GAMES OF 1976 were hit by a wave of political turmoil. Although rugby as a sport was not affiliated to the Olympic movement, the fact that the New Zealand All Blacks had recently toured South Africa was seen as an issue. Hundreds of black South Africans had been shot at a student protest in Soweto causing Tanzanian president Julius Nyerere to call for New Zealand's exclusion from the games. When the IOC would not capitulate, twenty-seven African nations elected to withdraw.

Under pressure from powerful Communist China, the weak willed Canadian government revoked the visas of the Taiwanese team who were already resident in the Olympic village. Despite protestation from the IOC the Taiwanese returned home. In reaction to the IOC's stand the Chinese failed to attend.

Montreal's Olympic project was grand to the extreme but poor financial planning and management coupled with a series of industrial disputes saw cost spiral from an estimated to $124 million to in excess of $2 billion, the Olympic stadium itself costing $485 million even with its roof unfinished.

Uniquely, the Olympic flame was "transmitted" by satellite from Athens to Ottawa where a laser bean was used

ABOVE Queen Elizabeth II opening the 1976 Montreal Olympics

In spite of the absentees from the African nations the level of competition was high. Of the 26 contested, new world records were set in 21 swimming events and tied in one more. The split of these medals was clear. In the men's events 12 of the 13 events were won by American swimmers whilst in the women's competition 11 titles went to East Germany. Having competitively come from nowhere there were suspicions, later confirmed, that the East German athletes were involved in the use of performance enhancing drugs.

Nadia Comaneci, a petite 14 year old Romanian, lit up the games with her gymnastic performances. With her trademark smile in place she completed an outstanding routine on the asymmetric bars and then stood anxiously watching for her score. It was a 10.0. A perfect score, awarded for the first time in Olympic competition. Comaneci proceeded to score a further six 10.0s on the way to winning three gold medals, one silver and one bronze.

ABOVE Interior of the Montreal Olympic swimming pool

to light the torch to be carried to Montreal. At the opening ceremony, in the presence of Queen Elizabeth II, the Olympic flame was lit by athletes Sandra Henderson and Stéphane Préfontaine. A few days later a torrential rainstorm doused the flames resulting in an official relighting the eternal Olympic symbol with his cigarette lighter!

Moscow 1980

IN DECEMBER 1979 SOVIET TROOPS invaded Afghanistan provoking anger and condemnation throughout the world. This anger manifested itself in no one more than US President Jimmy Carter. An election looming close, Carter instigated a campaign to boycott the imminent Moscow Olympics. Global opinion was mixed. Many nations wanted a complete boycott whilst others wanted to participate. A third group of nations including Great Britain, France and Spain wanted to compete without national emblems.

The games opened on 19 July 1980, the Olympic flame being lit by Russian basketball star Serge Belov. There was no coincidence in the choosing of Belov as it was he who had scored the controversial winning point in the 1976 final against the undefeated USA team.

Only 81 nations were represented, the lowest number since the Melbourne Games of 1956, but the quality of performance was exceptionally high as 34 world records and 62 Olympic records were broken.

Russian gymnast Nikolai Andrianov

won five medals taking his career total to 15 medals, seven of them gold. This astounding feat was soon eclipsed by his compatriot Aleksandr Dityatin who, by winning a medal in every men's gymnastic event, became the only athlete in history to win eight medals at one Olympics.

Building on their success at the Montreal Games, the East German women's swimming team dominated in the pool winning 11 of the 13

ABOVE Sebastian Coe of Great Britain leads team mates Steve Cram and Steve Ovett in the final of the 1500 metres

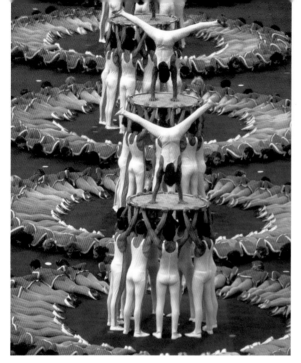

Having avoided each other in the heats and semi-finals of the 800 metres, their first meeting came at the final. A lap into the race Ovett found himself boxed in and back in sixth place with Coe trailing the field. Elbows flying and on the verge of disqualification, Ovett pushed his way to second place whilst Coe wasted time going round the field. Ovett then made his move and with 70m to go was clear of the field. Coe pressed on, out-sprinting Belarusian Nikolai Kirov for second place, three metres behind a victorious Ovett. Despite taking the silver medal, Coe considered this the most disappointing day of his athletic career.

The tables would be turned six days later as the two athletes met again in the final of the 1500 metres where Ovett was by far the favoured athlete having won 42 consecutive races at the distance. Coe, determined to avoid a repeat of his tactical disaster in the 800 metres matched Ovett stride for stride. In the final curve Coe unleashed his sprint, passing East German Jürgen Straub. Ovett responded but was no match for Coe's 12.1 second final 100 metres finishing third behind Straub. Coe had got his revenge and a deserved gold medal.

competitions. Russian swimmer Vladimir Salnikov became the first athlete ever to break fifteen minutes for 1500 metres on his way to collecting three gold medals.

British World record holder Sebastian Coe arrived at the Olympics firm favourite to win the 800 metres. His arch rival, fellow Briton Steve Ovett declared himself 90% certain to win at his favoured distance, the 1500 metres.

Moses

WHEN 20 YEAR OLD EDWIN MOSES arrived in Montreal to run in the 1976 Olympic 400 metres hurdles, few would have known that prior to 27 March of that same year he had only competed at that distance once in his life. A physics and engineering student at Atlanta's Morehouse College, Moses coached himself using local high school facilities as his own college had no track of its own.

With Ugandan reigning world record holder John Akii-Bua forced to stay away as part of the African Nations boycott and Great Britain's Alan Pascoe still suffering the effects of a leg injury the relatively unknown Moses grabbed his chance for Olympic glory. Using his unique 13 step stride pattern he demolished the field winning by an enormous 8 metres and setting a new world record time of 47.63 seconds.

Unable to compete at the Moscow Games of 1980, Moses returned to Olympic competition in Los Angeles. Between August 1977 and the start of the 1984 Games he had competed in 102 races, winning every one of them. An unquestionable favourite, Moses

lived up to expectations taking his second Olympic gold medal despite being heavily distracted at the start by the clicking of camera shutters.

Moses final Olympic appearance was at the Seoul Games of 1988. In a close competition he was relegated to a bronze medal having been outrun for gold by compatriot Danny Harris, the Olympic silver medallist in 1984 and the first athlete to break Moses' winning streak a year earlier.

ABOVE Ed Moses in action during the Mens 400 metres Hurdles

Munich 1972

RIGHT Valery Borzov
winning the Gold Medal
in the men's 100 metres

RIGHT Valery Borzov winning the Gold Medal in the men's 100 metres

FOR ALL THEIR ATHLETIC SUCCESS, the Berlin Olympics of 1936 are forever tainted by the dark shadow of Nazi Germany. It is difficult to look at a photograph of those Games without your attention being drawn to a military uniform or a swastika flag. As the opening of the 1972 Munich Games drew near the German nation, all too aware of these connotations, set to ensuring these games would be the greatest in history.

On 26 August 1972 the Games of the XX Olympiad were declared open as German athlete Gunther Zahn lit the Olympic flame. With 7,173 athletes from 121 nations attending, a record on both counts, it seemed that the German organisers had achieved their goal. The games continued in peace and harmony for a further nine days until the early hours of 5 September.

Between the hours of four and five, members of the Palestinian terrorist organisation Black September entered an apartment building at 31 Connolly Straße in the Olympic Village. It was here that members of the Israeli team were sleeping. As the terrorists stormed the accommodation wrestling trainer Moshe Weinberger was gunned down and killed. Weightlifter Yossef Romano was then shot as he tried to raise the alarm. Romano died later that day from his wounds. Only three Israeli athletes managed to escape, the remaining nine athletes and officials were taken hostage.

The terrorists published their demands – the unconditional release of 234 Palestinians detained in Israel and safe passage for themselves out of Germany. Avery Brundage, chairman of the I.O.C. announced "The Games must go on" but, with the situation worsening, competition was suspended at 3:51pm.

Negotiations took place all through the day then finally, at 10:10pm, the terrorists and their hostages emerged from the apartments to board a waiting coach which in turn transported them to three nearby helicopters. As the helicopters took off the German authorities entered the building to find the body of Weinberger and three Palestinian's suffering from serious stab wounds.

The helicopters flew to meet a waiting Boeing 727 at Füerstenfeldbruck military airbase. Once on the ground, as the terrorists ushered their prisoners towards the waiting airliner, concealed German snipers opened fire. The intention was simple: kill the terrorists and free the hostages. Despite early reports to the contrary, things had gone badly wrong. In the gun battle that followed, all nine Israeli athletes, five terrorists and a policeman were killed. Incredibly, considering the location and the security involved, three members of Black September escaped.

The next day a crowd of 80,000 attended a memorial service at the Olympic stadium. Avery Brundage insisted that "Peace must prevail over violence" so it was announced that the games would continue one day behind schedule.

In spite of the horrific events of 5 September there were some true athletic highlights at the Munich Games. Within a single week 22 year old

ABOVE One of the Black September guerrillas who broke into the Munich Olympic Village, killed two members of the Israeli team and took nine others hostage. Eventually all the hostages were killed after a pitched battle at Munich Airport

American swimmer Mark Spitz won an incredible seven gold medals with a world record time in each event. This success took his career Olympic medal tally to 11 medals, nine of them gold.

A 17 year old Belarusian, Olga Korbut, won the hearts of all who watched her as she recovered from failure to take two gold medals and one silver in the Gymnastics competition. Another young athlete, West German Ulrike Meyfarth, won the women's high jump competition at the age of 16 becoming the youngest winner of an individual athletics event in Olympic history.

Chaos and controversy reigned supreme as the USA and the USSR met in the basketball final. With three second remaining a trailing USA were awarded two free throws. Both scored and the Americans took the lead 50-49. With a single second remaining Soviet coach Vladimir Kondrashkin ran to the referee insisting that he had called a time-out and had not been heard. At the insistence the FIBA chairman a time-out was given but as the two seconds had not been put back on the clock the buzzer immediately sounded. The Americans were jubilant, their fans invading the court. However, the FIBA

chairman once again intervened insisting the missing three seconds be put back on the clock. The time was reset allowing the Russians to inbound the ball straight to Aleksandr Belov who scored unopposed. For the first time ever the American basketball team had been defeated.

Nurmi

KNOWN AS "THE PHANTOM FINN", Paavo Nurmi was born in Turku in June 1897. An athlete of incredible endurance, Nurmi dominated middle and long distance running in the 1920s always competing with a stopwatch in his hand.

Nurmi's inaugural Olympics were the 1920 Antwerp Games. Competing in his first event, the 5,000 metres, he was out-sprinted in the last 200 metres by Frenchman Joseph Guillemot but managed to collect a silver medal as consolation. Three days later the tables were turned as Nurmi won a gold medal in the 10,000 metres with rival Guillemot taking the silver. Competing in the now discontinued cross-country he won his third and fourth gold medals in the individual and team competitions.

Nurmi achieved an incredible feat at the 1924 Paris Games. Setting off at a blistering pace he set an Olympic record time in the 1500 metres to take the gold medal then, just one hour later, returned to the track to take victory in the 5,000 metres. Later in the competition Nurmi won three more gold medals taking victory in the 3,000 metres team race and both individual and team honours in the cross country.

Nurmi's final Olympic appearance was in Amsterdam at the 1928 Games where he achieved his ninth gold medal by winning the 10,000 metres and silver medals in the 5,000 metres and the 3,000 metres steeplechase.

Paavo Nurmi's record of nine career Olympic gold medals is shared only by three other athletes and bettered by none.

Oldest and Youngest

BELOW Oscar Swahn, the oldest person ever to win an Olympic medal

GREEK DIMITRIOUS LOUNDROUS was only 10 years 218 days when he finished third in the team parallel bars at the 1896 Games and Italy's Luigina Giavotta, won a women's team gymnastics silver medal in 1928 aged just 11 years 302 days. There is though a mystery surrounding the identity of a young Parisian boy. Drafted in at the last moment, he coxed Dutch rowers Roelof Klein and François Antoine Brandt to victory in the coxed pairs competition at the 1900 Paris Games and then, after posing for a victory photograph disappeared back to the streets of Paris.

American springboard diver Marjorie Gestring, at 13 years and 268 days, remains the youngest ever Olympic individual gold medallist. Kusuo Kitamura of Japan hold the record as the youngest ever male Olympic individual gold medallist being only 14 years 309 days old when taking victory in the 1500 metre final at the 1932 Games.

Oscar Swahn on Sweden became the oldest ever Olympic gold medallist winning the team single-shot running deer shooting in 1912 at the age of 64 years 257 days. Astoundingly Swahn returned to the Games in Antwerp to take a silver medal in the same event making him, at 72 years 279 days, the oldest Olympic competitor ever.

The oldest female competitor was Lorna Johnstone who, at the age of 70 years and 5 days, competed for the Great Britain equestrian dressage team at the Munich Games of 1972.

On Target

TWO FORMS OF TARGET SPORT ARE contested at the Olympic Games – archery and shooting.

Archery first appeared as part of the Olympic programme at the 1900 Paris Games and then again in 1904, 1908 and 1920 before being discontinued. It reappeared on the schedule at the 1972 Munich Games with team events being added in 1988.

Modern bows are of a composite construction combining wood, ceramic, carbon fibre, foam or fibre glass, and are permitted to have non-magnifying sights and stabilising weights. The arrows are steel tipped shafts of carbon fibre or aluminium with a fletching to assist flight.

Olympic archery targets are 1.22 metres in diameter and stand 1.3 metres from the ground. The face of the target is has coloured concentric rings, the inner gold zone being worth 10 points, the outer gold worth 9 points and so on down to the outer white circle which is worth 1 point.

The format of the archery competition has undergone great change since its reintroduction to the Games. The current system is the simplest with the 64 entrants first shooting a qualifying round of 72 arrows. All competitors then advance to match play of 18 arrows with the highest scoring archer playing the lowest scoring. This is repeated until the quarter finals at which point each round is contested with just 12 arrows through to the final.

Shooting has appeared at every Olympics with the exception of the

BELOW Richard Brickell of Great Britain shoots during the men's skeet qualifying event in Athens 2004

1904 St. Louis Games. Early Olympic shooting events included classes for weapons such as the military revolver and military rifle and even the duelling pistol in which competitors fired on life sized dummies dressed in frock coats. In the 1900 Paris Games there was even an event that involved shooting at live pigeons!

There are three basic forms of shooting in Olympic competition – pistol, rifle and clay. Each competition takes the form of a preliminary round followed by a shootout final to decide the medals. In 1996 the open format of competition with men competing against women was discarded in favour of separate men's and women's competitions.

For rifle and pistol shooting events, targets vary in size but all feature concentric rings scoring 1 point for the outer through to 10 points for a bullseye. The distance of the target varies between 10 and 50 metres depending on the weapon used.

Skeet shooting and trap shooting using a .12 gauge shotgun make up the clay competitions. In a trap event, clays are launched at predetermined angles with the shooter allowed two shots at each. The shooter in a skeet competition must hold his shotgun at waist level until the clay is released. Unlike trap shooting in which all clays are launched from ground level, skeet clays may be set from a high or a low tower.

Owens

JESSE OWENS IS AN OLYMPIC legend. Born in Alabama he first came to athletic prominence aged 21 when, at the Michigan Big Ten Championships he broke five world records and equalled a sixth within the space of 45 minutes.

His most famous achievements occurred at the 1936 Berlin Olympics in the heart of Nazi Germany and the presence of Adolf Hitler. Owens breezed through the qualifying heats of the 100 metres, tying the Olympic record in the first round. In the final he fought off a strong challenge from countryman Ralph Metcalfe to take the gold medal in 10.3 seconds.

Qualification for the long jump was not as easy with Owens fouling his first two attempts. Approached by German Luz Long, a suggestion was made that if he took off early he could still easily make the distance. Taking the advice of his rival he qualified by just one centimetre. Matching each other jump for jump in the final, it took an enormous 8.06 metres leap by Owens to secure the gold medal from Long.

Competing in the 200 metres final

Owens controlled the race from start to finish and was barely challenged as he sped his way to a third gold medal of the Games.

A fourth gold medal was easily won in the 4x100 metres relay despite controversy surrounding Owens' and Metcalfe's last minute selection over Marty Glickman and Sam Stoller, the only two Jewish athletes on the US track team.

Owens astonishing and symbolic achievement in the heart of Nazi Germany remains one of the most endearing images in Olympic history.

ABOVE Jesse Owens captures the gold in the long jump event during Olympic Games in Berlin 1936

Paris 1900

RIGHT A portrait of British tennis player Charlotte Cooper

FOLLOWING THE UNDISPUTED success of the 1896 Athens Games a large number of people shared an opinion that the Greek capital should play host to the Olympic Games on a permanent basis. But under pressure from president and founder of the modern Olympic movement, Baron de Coubertin, the International Olympic Committee agreed that the 1900 Games should be awarded to Paris as part of the World Fair.

Seen as a supporting event and with competition spread from July to October, the Games were referred to as the "Paris Championships" – many competitors lived and died unaware that they had participated in the Olympics. The Games though, were not entirely without highlights.

A 23 year old American, Alvin Kraenzheim, would become the first Olympian to win four gold medals by taking the 60 metres sprint, 100 metres and 200 metres hurdles and the long jump - controversially as his prime adversary, fellow American Meyer Prinstein, refused to jump in the Sunday final as it fell on a Sunday.

Fast times were the order of the day in the swimming events, largely due to the fact that they took place in the River Seine with the current! Women would compete in the Games for the first time with British tennis player Charlotte Cooper becoming the inaugural female Champion.

Paris 1924

THE PARIS GAMES OF 1924 SAW THE French capital hosting 3092 athletes representing 44 nations over 126 events in 19 sports. For the first time athletes were accommodated in an Olympic Village. Another first was the introduction of the Olympic motto "Citius, Altius, Fortius" – Swifter, Higher, Stronger.

Competing in the long jump, University of Michigan student William DeHart Hubbard became the first black athlete to win an Olympic gold medal. Unfortunately his efforts were somewhat eclipsed by those of fellow American Robert LeGendre who, having failed to qualify for the U.S. long jump team, set a new world record of 25 feet 5 inches the previous day whilst competing in the pentathlon.

Finland's Paavo Nurmi took the headlines by winning an astonishing five gold medals. His performance is all the more amazing considering there was only a gap of 55 minutes between him finishing the 5000m and taking to the start of the 5000m.

Several athletes competing at the Games are known for going on to other endeavours. U.S. double gold medallist Johnny Weissmuller would head to Hollywood to star as Tarzan in 12 movies whilst rowing gold medallist Ben Spock would achieve fame with his book The Common Sense Book of Baby and Child Care.

BELOW The first ever Olympic Village, built for the 1924 games in Paris.

Pentathlon

RIGHT The start of the men's swimming event of the modern pentathlon during the Athens 2004 Olympic Games

BELOW Zsuzsanna Voros of Hungary with her horse Guelfo del Belagaio competes in the riding discipline of the Modern Pentathlon during the 2004 Olympic Games in Athens

THE MODERN PENTATHLON, contested by both men and women, was devised by Olympic founder Baron Pierre de Coubertin who had been fascinated by the pentathlon of the ancient Games in which an athlete would run, jump, throw a javelin and a discus and then wrestle. A test of a true soldier! In updating the event de Coubertin retained the premise that the competitor was a soldier but in this case his task was to deliver a message.

He starts his mission on horseback but is forced onto foot where he duels with the sword. To escape he must shoot with a pistol and swim across a river before running back to camp through the woods.

In competition an Olympic modern pentathlon competitor must first fire twenty shots from an air pistol at a target 10 metres distant. They then fence every other competitor in fast one minute bouts, the first scoring a hit being declared the winner. Next is a 300 metres freestyle pool swim followed later by a single round of show jumping on an unfamiliar horse. Pentathletes are given just 20 minutes to get to know the horse, and for the horse to get to know them! The final event is a 3,000 metres cross country run.

Points are awarded depending on how the athlete's performance compares to a standard set for each element of the competition.

Quick off the Blocks

SEEN AS THE PREMIERE EVENT OF the Olympic Games, the 100 metres never fails to capture the imagination. An event of outright power, athletes do not even take time to breathe from the moment the gun fires until they have crossed the finish line.

The first Olympic 100 metres Champion was American Thomas Burke. Victorious with a 12.0 seconds run, he had wowed a curious Greek pubic with his pioneering crouched start position.

Great Britain won its first Olympic 100 metres at the 1924 Paris Games. Immortalised in the film Chariots of Fire, Harold Abrahams, having hired the services of legendary coach Harold Mussabini, stormed to victory, equalling the Olympic record of 10.6 seconds.

The eventful 1936 Olympics saw the powerful Nazi propaganda machine confounded by the 100 metres triumph of African-American Jesse Owens to the delight of the Berlin crowd.

Assisted by the rarefied atmosphere of the Mexico City Stadium, American James Hines sped to victory in a word record time of 9.95 seconds at the 1968 Games. His time would not be bettered in Olympic competition until Carl Lewis recorded 9.90 seconds at the 1988 Seoul Games following Canadian Ben Johnson's disqualification drug use.

Britain's Linford Christie, at 32 years old, became the oldest ever winner of the 100 metres at the 1992 Barcelona Olympics recording 9.96 seconds. Canadian Donovan Bailey's Atlanta Games performance of 9.84 seconds in 1996 set a new world record and remains the fastest 100 metres performance in Olympic history.

BELOW Donovan Baily, winning the men's 100m in a new world record of 9.84 seconds at the Olympic Stadium at the 1996 Centennial Olympic Games in Atlanta, Georgia

Racket Sports

THREE FORMS OF RACKET SPORT
are contested at the Olympic Games –
tennis, table tennis and badminton.

Tennis first featured in the
Olympics at the Athens Games of
1896 with a women's competition
being added in 1900. Charlotte
Cooper of Great Britain, a five times
Wimbledon Champion, was not only

the first winner of the women's tennis
tournament but also the first female
Champion of the modern Olympics.
Despite its popularity, tennis was
dropped from the programme following the Paris Games of 1924 due to
issues of professionalism. It would be
another sixty years before tennis
would again feature at the Olympics,
first as a demonstration sport in 1984
and then as a full medal sport in 1988
at which point professionals were permitted to take part.

Germany's Steffi Graff, winner of
the 1984 demonstration tournament
despite being its youngest competitor,
arrived at the 1988 Olympic Games
ranked number one in the world. That
year she had won the Australian Open,
French Open, Wimbledon and, just a
week prior to the Games, the US open.
To this she added an Olympic gold

medal, beating Argentinean Gabriella Sabatini in straight sets.

Considering the Asian nations' passion for the game of table tennis, it seems appropriate that its inclusion in the Olympics commenced at the 1988 Seoul Games. To the delight of a more than enthusiastic home crowd, the first men's singles final was an all-Korean affair between Yoo Nam-Kyu and Kim Ki-Taik. Asian dominance of the sport was further demonstrated in the women's singles competition at the 1996 Atlanta Games at which 11 of the 63 competitors were of Chinese birth.

Although it remains a topic of debate, it is said that the sport of badminton was invented in the mid 1800s at Badminton House in Gloucestershire although the location is now more readily associated with equestrianism. Badminton made an appearance as a demonstration sport at the 1972 Munich Games before gaining acceptance as a full Olympic sport for male and female competitors at Barcelona

in 1992. Matches are played as the best of three sets, a set being won by the first player to reach 15 points in men's and doubles competition or 11 points in the women's competition.

BELOW Korea's Yoo Nam Kiu hits a forehand during the men's table tennis final at the Olympic Games in Seoul. Yoo Nam Kiu won the gold medal

Redgrave

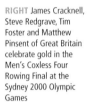

WHEN A 22 YEAR OLD Steve Redgrave rowed to an Olympic gold medal as a member of the coxed fours at the 1984 Los Angeles Games few would have realised that in twenty years time he would be considered Britain's greatest ever Olympian.

Born in Buckinghamshire, Redgrave was always seen as being single minded in his quest for success. His ability to work through pain and beyond his own physical threshold has set him apart from other athletes who could only hope to emulate his drive and determination.

Paired with Andrew Holmes, Redgrave achieved his second Olympic gold medal in the coxless pairs at the 1988 Seoul Games. Less than 24 hours later he and Holmes rowed to a bronze medal in the coxed pairs.

Redgrave returned from the 1992 Barcelona Games with a third gold medal having partnered Matthew Pinsent to victory in the coxless pairs. In doing so he had become only the third British athlete to earn gold medals in three consecutive Olympics. Partnered again by Pinsent he returned to Olympic competition in Atlanta to collect his fourth Olympic gold medal in their 100th race as a partnership following which he commented, "Anyone who sees me go anywhere near a boat again, ever, you've got my permission to shoot me".

Having been diagnosed with diabetes training became difficult for Redgrave but his determination won through and on 23 September 2000 Redgrave, Pinsent, James Cracknell and Tim Foster powered their way to victory over a closing Italian team in the final of the Olympic coxless fours. In doing so he became only the fourth athlete in history to win gold medals at five different Games.

Steve Redgrave is arguably Great Britain's greatest ever Olympian.

RIGHT James Cracknell, Steve Redgrave, Tim Foster and Matthew Pinsent of Great Britain celebrate gold in the Men's Coxless Four Rowing Final at the Sydney 2000 Olympic Games

BELOW Steve Redgrave of Great Britain holds his Five Olympic Gold Medals

Relatively Speaking

THERE IS A LONG HISTORY OF BOTH rivalry and cooperation amongst relatives at the Olympics. At the inaugural Athens Games in 1896 American brothers John and Sumner Paine finished first and second in the military revolver shooting. Four years later in Paris, the Doherty brothers representing Great Britain were due to meet in the semi finals of the men's singles tennis competition. Reginald stepped aside, forfeiting the match and allowing his brother Laurie to rest for the final which he subsequently won. Reginald then defeated Arthur Norris in the minor final to take the bronze medal. Both players then went forward to win the doubles competition.

During the Antwerp Games of 1920 Italian fencer Neo Nadi won an astounding five gold medals whilst his younger brother Aldo collected three gold medals and one silver.

American rower Bill Havens forfeited his seat in the coxed eights at the 1924 Games to stay at home with his pregnant wife. In 1952, Frank Havens, the son born during those Olympics, won a gold medal in the 10,000 metres Canadian singles canoeing whilst at the 1948 Games the star-class yachting was won by fellow Americans father and son Hillary and Paul Smart.

A true family effort was displayed in the cycling team time trial at the 1968 Games during which Swedish brothers Erik, Gösta, Sture and Tomas Pettersson secured silver medals.

BELOW The Italian Fencing team including Aldo Nadi (centre left) and Nedo Nadi (centre right) posing during the 1920 Olympic Games in Antwerp, Belgium

Rome 1960

THE 1960 ROME GAMES WERE TO
be a proud moment for the Italian capital. The Vesuvius eruption of 1906 had
meant that the planned Rome Games of
1908 had been cancelled and reassigned
to London. With typical Italian style,
and the obligatory blessing from Pope
John XXIII, the Italians presented an
Olympic showcase of epic proportion.

Wrestlers competed in the Basilica de
Maxentius where bouts had been fought
two millennia before whilst gymnasts
performed in the ancient Caracalla Baths.

The fourth-century Arch of
Constantine would provide the stunning backdrop for the finish of the
marathon – the first to be run at night.
With the way lit by torches
held by Italian soldiers it
was here that barefoot
Ethiopian Abebe Bikila took
Olympic marathon victory
and in doing so became the
first black African Olympic
gold medallist.

A resurging German team
surprised many by beating
the United States in the rowing coxed eights and on the
track in the 4x100m relay.
America had won every
Olympic final in both events
since 1920. To cap these fine
performances another
German, Armin Hary, beat
American David Sime to
win the blue riband 100
metre sprint.

Rowing

ROWING HAS BEEN AN OLYMPIC sport since the Paris Games of 1900 with women's events being introduced to the programme at the Montreal Games of 1976. Over the years the competition distance has changed several times until 2,000 metres was agreed for both men's and women's competition at the 1992 Barcelona Games.

There are two types of rowing contested at Olympic competition – sculls and sweeps. Sculls are contested individually, as pairs and as fours by both men and women (albeit in separate competitions) with each sculler pulling a pair of 2.98 metre sculling blades. Sweeps are raced in pairs and eights by women and men and as fours by men only. In all variations the rowers pull a 3.82 metres long single oar with its blade painted in the national colours of the team.

BELOW James Cracknell, Steve Redgrave, Tim Foster and Matthew Pinsent of Great Britain cross the line to win Gold in the Men's Coxless Four Rowing Final ahead of Italy (Silver) and Australia (Bronze)

The men's eight also requires the use of a coxswain whose job it is to steer the boat. There is a minimum weight for coxswains of 55 kilograms. If a coxswain is found to be underweight, ballast may be added to remove any advantage in the water.

In 1996 a lightweight class was added to the programme with a lightweight coxless four for men and lightweight double-sculls competitions for men and women. To qualify for the light weight class rowers must weigh no more that 72.5 kilograms for men and 59 kilograms for women but in addition the average weight of the crew may not exceed 70 kilograms for men's crews and 57 kilograms for women's.

The rowing competitions comprise of a qualifying round from which the fastest twelve boats progress to the semi finals. The three fastest semi-finalists in each round move forward to take part in the final with the remaining six teams contest a "petit final" to establish positions down to twelfth place.

Seoul 1988

IT HAS BEEN SAID THAT POLITICS have a detrimental effect on the Olympics. In the case of the 1988 Seoul Games there was a clear demonstration on how the Olympics can have a positive effect on politics. In order to satisfy international opinion and with the eyes of the world watching, the ruling South Korean dictatorship abdicated in favour of democratic elections.

Great drama surrounded the opening ceremony. The Olympic torch entered the stadium in the hand of 76 year old Sohn Kee-chung, winner of the marathon at the 1936 Berlin Games where, due to the military occupation of Korea, he had been forced to run under the Japanese name of Son Kitei. Far from showing his advancing years Sohn sprinted into the stadium filled with pride.

Making its Olympic appearance for the first time, the table tennis competi-tion was dominated by the host nation and the Chinese. On the grass courts, ten-nis made a return to the games after a 64 year absence bring-ing with it some of the biggest names in the sport - singles gold medals being awarded to Slovakian Miloslav Mečíř in the men's tourna-ment and West Germany's Steffi Graf in the women's.

East German Kristin Otto caused a sensation in the pool, winning six gold medals with victories in the 50m and 100m freestyle, 100m backstroke, 100m butterfly, 4x100 freestyle and 4x100 medley. As Otto had dominated the women's swimming events so six-foot six-inch American Matt Biondi would dominate the men's competition. In an

outstanding series of performances, Biondi won seven medals, five of them gold, taking the top spot on the rostrum in the 50m and 100m freestyle, 4x100m and 4x200m relays and the 4x100m medley.

Further excitement poolside was generated by diver Greg Louganis of the United States who became the first man in Olympic history to win both the springboard and platform diving competitions despite hitting his head against the board during the preliminary rounds.

By far the biggest story of the 1988 Games was that of Canadian sprinter Ben Johnson who, after setting a new world record in the final of the 100 metres sprint, tested positive for the banned steroid Stanozolol. Although there had been positive tests in previous Olympic Games this was the first time such a major name had been caught. Johnson returned to Canada in disgrace with Carl Lewis of the United States being awarded the gold medal.

In the women's track competition American Florence Griffith-Joyner, known as Flo-Jo, took victory first in the 100m, then the 200m recording world record times in the semi-final and final, achieving a third gold medal in the 4x100m relay.

Setting Sail

SAILING IS THE ONLY OLYMPIC sport in which men and women are permitted to compete against each other. Competitors sail in a series of races with points being awarded depending on their placing. The first place crew scores 1 point , the second placed 2 points and so on. The crew with the lowest cumulative score wins the competition.

The classes of craft used in Olympic Sailing are divided into four groups – windsurfer, dinghy, keel boat and catamaran.

Windsurfing was first introduced into the Games in 1984. Currently this class utilises the Mistral One type of board, a 1.24 metre long board topped with a 7.4 square metre sail.

The dinghy category utilises the single sail (una) rigged Finn, Europe and Laser classes and the two sail (sloop) rigged 49er and 470 classes. Dinghies are steered by a rudder with the crew using body weight to counterbalance the craft.

The Solling and Star classes are categorised as keel boats, named after the ballasted fin fixed to the hull. The

Solling, requiring a crew of three, is the largest craft used in Olympic sailing at 8.2 metres in length.

The Tornado is the only catamaran used in Olympic competition. These are twin hulled craft with a sloop rig and a fixed mainsail and are the fastest of the sailing classes with the exception of the windsurfers.

ABOVE John Lovell and Charlie Ogeltree of USA in action sail their way to silver in the open multihull tornado finals race 4 during the Athens 2004 Summer Olympic Games

Spitz

CALIFORNIAN MARK SPITZ MADE
his inaugural Olympic appearance at
the Mexico City Games of 1968.
Buoyed by an impressive six gold

medal Pan American Games winning
streak he had great plans to repeat
the feat in the Olympic pool.
Ambition was outstripped by ability
with Spitz only taking gold medals in
the 4x100 metres and 4x200 metres
relays, a silver medal in the 100m

butterfly and a bronze medal in the 100m freestyle.

For the 1972 Munich Games Spitz set himself three goals; to become the first swimmer to win five gold medals at one Olympics, the first athlete to win six gold medals at one Olympics and to do even better and win seven gold medals.

Spitz opened his campaign in phenomenal form winning the 200 metres butterfly by over two seconds. On the same day he won his second gold medal in the 4x100 metres freestyle. Back in the water the next day Spitz made it three, winning the 200 metres freestyle. After a days rest he then took gold medals in the 100 metres butterfly and in the 4x200 metres freestyle by almost five seconds. His greatest challenge came in the 100m freestyle. Pitted against in-form American Jerry Heidenreich, Spitz went hard from the gun. Almost floundering in the last strokes he held on to take his sixth gold. Almost a formality, Spitz collected his seventh gold medal in the 4x100 metres medley.

Spitz had not only set a currently unbroken record by winning seven gold medals at one Olympic Games he had also set a new world record time in all seven events.

St Louis 1904

LESSONS SHOULD HAVE BEEN learned from the 1900 Paris Games debacle but it was not to be. Awarded to Chicago as a reward for American athletes support of the 1896 and 1900 Games, the 1904 Games should have gone well. The city of St. Louis, scheduled to hold its own world's fair, had other plans and threatened to organise a rival international sporting competition. Under pressure from U.S. president Theodore Roosevelt the IOC reluctantly agreed to move the games.

Once again events were spread over several months and were nowhere to be found amongst the frenzy of the world's fair. Many European athletes stayed away and of the 84 events scheduled a mere 42 included competitors from outside North America.

Despite all its difficulties there were again some remarkable performances. Tswana tribesmen Jan Mashiani and Len Tau were the first African athletes to compete having found themselves in St. Louis only as part of the fair's Boer War exhibit. High jumper Joseph Stadler and hurdler George Poage became the first African-American athletes to win medals.

American gymnast George Eyser remarkably won three gold, two silver and one bronze medal, a fact made even more impressive as he competed with a wooden leg having been run over by a train.

Stockholm 1912

MANY NEW INNOVATIONS WERE brought to the fore at the Stockholm Games of 1912. Electronic timing devices were used, albeit unofficially, for the track events and a public address system kept spectators and competitors informed of events.

Women's swimming was introduced for the first time with Australian Sarah "Fanny" Durack claiming victory in the 100m freestyle despite having been required to cover her own expenses to attend. Success in the women's 4x100m freestyle relay would go to the British team of Isabella Moore, Jennie Fletcher, Annie Speirs and Irene Steer.

Two battles of epic proportions were fought in the Greco-Roman wrestling tournament. Finland's Ivar Böling and Swede Anders Ahlgren grappled for an incredible nine hours in the light-heavyweight final before judges declared a draw. Olympic rules stated that it was necessary for a winner to defeat his adversary so it was decided that both men would be awarded silver medals.

A semi-final bout in the middleweight category would see Estonian Martin Klein and Finn Alfred Asikainen wrestle for eleven hours before Klein would eventually pin his opponent and take the win. Unfortunately the effort had exhausted him so much that he was unable to take part in the final, victory going to Swedish competitor Claes Johanson by default.

BELOW A general view of the stadium used for the 1912 Stockholm Olympics

Sydney 2000

IMMACULATELY CONCEIVED AND executed, the Sydney 2000 Olympics came as a welcome tonic after the poorly organised and overtly commercialised Atlanta Games four years previously. The Australian population understood the importance of the millennium Games in the eyes of the world and in return presented an Olympic experience bigger, brighter and better than any that had gone before.

RIGHT Horseriders carry Olympic flags during the opening ceremony of the Sydney 2000 Olympic Games

BELOW Jonathan Edwards celebrates Gold in the Triple Jump final

199 nations, the greatest number ever, were represented by a record 10,651 athletes competing in 300 events across 29 sports. 47,000 volunteers kept the Games ticking like clockwork whilst 16,000 accredited members of the media kept a global audience informed.

In an impressive opening ceremony display, 120 Australian stock-horses performed to a capacity crowd in the 110,000 seat purpose built Olympic stadium before Kathy Freeman, an Australian athlete of Aboriginal descent, lit the Olympic flame.

Freeman filled the spotlight again just ten days later during what turned out to be one of the greatest nights in athletic history by winning the women's 400 metres final by four metres from Jamaican Lorraine Graham in front of a crowd of 112,524. In the next race American Michael Johnson took victory in the 400 metres becoming the Games first repeat winner at the distance. Britain's Jonathan Edwards won the triple jump after a disappointing performance in Atlanta and Maria Mutola of Mozambique, competing in her fourth Games, snatched victory in the women's 800m to win her first Olympic gold medal.

records in the space of one hour. The first saw him win the 400 metres by almost three seconds from Italian Massimiliano Rosolino, the second, as part of the Australian 4x100 metres relay team, put an end to the United States' unbeaten record in the event. More was expected of "the Thorpedo" in the 200 metres freestyle but the gold medal was won by 22 year old Dutchman Pieter Van den Hoogenband who in doing so set a world record for himself. Just two days later Van den Hoogenband completed a medal double by defeating Russian great Aleksandr Popov in the 100 metres freestyle.

For Great Britain the most outstanding moment of the games came on 23 September. With the entire nation watching on television, the team of James Cracknell, Tim Foster, Matthew Pinsent and Steve Redgrave rowed their way to victory in the coxless fours. With this victory 38 year old Redgrave became only the fourth athlete ever to earn gold medals at five different Olympic Games.

The highlight of the evening was to be the final of the men's 10,000m. Ethiopian world record holder Haile Gabrselassie had not lost at the distance in seven years but had missed three month of preparation due to injury. An electrifying race ensued. At 250m to go Kenyan Paul Tergat raced to the front with Gabrselassie in pursuit until, with only 50m remaining, he pulled alongside Tergat. Tergat fought back, Gabrselassie holding level until his final strides when the Ethiopian dipped forward to take the gold medal by just nine-hundredths of a second.

Competing at his first Olympic Games, Australia's Ian Thorpe broke two world

BELOW Cathy Freeman cruises to victory to take the gold medal in a special body suit in the Women's 400m final

Team Sports

THERE ARE CURRENTLY SEVEN team sports contested in Olympic competition with men competing at baseball, women at softball and both sexes taking part in basketball, football, handball, hockey and volleyball.

Baseball was finally given the status of an Olympic medal sport at the 1992 Barcelona Games after having appeared as a demonstration sport on seven occasions since 1900. Olympic baseball is played over nine innings. Each team takes turns in batting and fielding, its turn in bat finishing when three players are deemed out. If the score is tied at the end of the ninth inning further innings are contested until a team takes the lead.

Qualification for the Olympics is through a series of regional tournaments that generate two teams from Asia, the Americas and Europe and one from a combined Oceania and Africa. In the Olympic competition itself each team plays the seven others once in a round-robin tournament. The top four teams advance to the semi-finals with the first placed team playing the fourth placed team and the second playing the third. The two winning teams then meet to contest the final for gold and solver medals whilst the losing teams play for the bronze.

Women's softball made its Olympic debut at the 1996 Atlanta Games.

ABOVE Action in the Women's beach volleyball competition during the 2004 Olympics in Athens

Softball is essentially the same as Baseball but there are some intrinsic differences such as the fact that the game is played over seven innings as opposed to nine and the pitcher, who stands 20 feet closer to the home plate than in baseball, must throw underhand rather than overhand. The ball itself differs considerably being both larger and heavier. Despite its name, softball should not be considered a soft game. One pitch at the 1996 Atlanta games was recorded at 118 kph (73.3 mph).

Baseball and Softball will be contested as Olympic medal sports for the last time at the Beijing Games in 2008 following a decision by the IOC to drop them from the programme.

Basketball made its first Olympic appearance at the 1936 Berlin Games in a tournament won, not surprisingly, by the United States of America. They continued to dominate the competition until the 1972 Munich Olympics at which a determined Soviet team inflicted defeat after controversially

ABOVE Grant Schubert of Australia scores on a high shot over the blocker of goaltender Bernardino Herrera of Spain in the men's field hockey semi-final during the Athens 2004 Olympic Games

teams who are, with the exception of the host nation and the reigning world Champions, required to qualify through a Championship the year preceding the Games.

Football has enjoyed a long existence in Olympic history. First appearing at the 1900 Paris Games it has featured at every Olympiad since with the exception of those held in Los Angeles in 1932. In 1996 a women's tournament was added to the programme which will be contested by twelve teams when the Games reach Beijing in 2008. Since 1992 professional players have been eligible to play in Olympic competition provided they are under 23 years old. A team may now also add to its squad a maximum of three professional players over this age restriction.

Handball made its Olympic debut at the 1936 Berlin Games although it did not make a second appearance until the 1972 Munich Games with the women's tournament being introduced in 1976. Handball is a fast moving game between two teams of seven players contested over two thirty minute halves. Much like basketball, players move the ball by passing and

scoring in the final seconds. In 1992 American dominance returned to the competition following a decision to allow professional players to participate. Women's basketball was introduced to the Games in 1976.

Olympic basketball is played over four ten minute periods with an additional five minute overtime period being allocated should the game be tied. Both the men's and the women's tournaments are contested by 12

dribbling but the object of the game is to score goals in a defended net rather than a suspended basket.

Hockey first became an Olympic sport at the 1908 London Games. For many years India dominated the tournament winning thirty consecutive games to claim six gold medals between 1928 and 1956. The women's hockey was introduced to the Games in 1980. Both the men's and the women's competitions start with a preliminary round with the teams split into two pools. The top two teams from each pool progress to the semi-finals whilst the remaining teams contest classification matches to establish the lesser placings. The winning semi-final teams advance to meet in the final to decide the gold and silver medals while the semi final losers play for the bronze.

Volleyball has been an Olympic sport since the introduction of men's and women's tournaments at the 1964 Tokyo Games. Twelve teams take part in each tournament with matches being played as the best of five sets. The first four sets of competition are played to 25 points with the final set being played to just 15 points although there must be a

clear two point advantage.

Although volleyball has always generated a strong following at the Olympics, the introduction of beach volleyball at the 1996 Atlanta Games has opened the sport to a whole new audience. Played in pairs rather than teams of twelve, beach volleyball players must have excellent coordination and stamina to cope with the difficult sandy playing surface.

ABOVE Argentina celebrate after beating Paraguay 1-0 to claim the men's football gold medal in Athens 2004

Thompson

RIGHT Daley
Thompson clears the
bar in the Pole Vault
section during the
Decathlon event at
the 1984 Olympic
Games

BELOW Jurgen
Hingsen (left) of
Germany and Daley
Thompson (right)
shake hands during
the medal ceremony
for the Decathlon
event in 1984

DALEY THOMPSON REMAINS ONE of the best loved characters in British Olympic history. His trademark moustache, beaming smile and pithy one liners endeared him to the public an fellow athletes alike. At 18 years old, Frances Morgan Thompson arrived at the 1976 Montreal Olympics the youngest decathlon competitor finishing eighteenth overall.

Four years later and Thompson had raised his game. The West German boycott of the Moscow Olympics had removed the threat of Guido Kratschmer, his greatest rival. With little opposition he set out at a blistering pace but heavy rain on the second day thwarted any hopes of a world record. Regardless, Thompson demolished the field finishing 164 points clear.

By the Los Angeles Games of 1984 Thompson had a new West German rival in the form of world record holder Jürgen Hingsen. Neck and neck, the crucial moment came as Thompson made two poor throws in the discus whereas Hingsen threw a huge 50.82 metres. Under pressure he replied with a 46.56 metre throw; enough to secure 100 points and maintain his lead. Competing in the pole vault Hingsen complained of feeling ill and underperformed. For Thompson victory was but a formality. Cruising home in the 1500m, he then took a victory lap wearing a t-shirt with the message "THANKS AMERICA FOR A GOOD GAMES AND A GREAT TIME", whilst on the back it read "BUT WHAT ABOUT THE TV COVERAGE?" – a reference to US television only covering the performances of American athletes.

Tokyo 1964

NINETEEN YEAR OLD JAPANESE athlete Yoshinori Sakai was chosen to light the Olympic flame at the commencement of the 1964 Tokyo Games. He had been born in Hiroshima on 6 August 1945, the day the first atomic bomb had been unleashed.

Judo found itself included in the program for the first time but to the surprise and embarrassment of the host nation the gold medal went to Antonius Geesink, a 267-pound 6-foot 6-inch judo instructor from Utrecht, Holland.

Ethiopia's Abebe Bikila retained his marathon title setting a new world record time in the process and competing less than six weeks after an appendix operation. Another athlete performing under duress was discus thrower Al Oerter of the United States who, suffering from torn rib cartilage and a cervical disc injury, was forced to wear a neck harness. Despite his discomfort Oerter threw 61 meters to take the gold medal and an Olympic record.

Ukrainian gymnast Larysa Latynina won six medals, two of each colour, to take her Olympic career total to a stunning 18 medals.

A somewhat unusual record was achieved in the semi-final of the cycling match sprint as Frenchman Pierre Trentin and Giovanni Pettenella of Italy balanced upright for 21 minutes 57 seconds without moving.

BELOW Antonius Geesink of Holland raises his arms in victory after beating Japan's Akio Kaminaga in the final of the Judo non-category class at the 1964 Tokyo Olympics

Track and Field

TRACK AND FIELD, OTHERWISE known as Athletics, is rightfully considered the backbone of the Olympics featuring, as it does, many of the Blue Riband events of the Games. Just twelve track and field events were contested at the 1896 Athens Olympics but by the time the Games returned to the Greek capital in 2004, this number had increased almost fourfold to 46 events.

Olympic track and field can be broken down in to six categories of event – sprints, middle distance, long distance, jumping, throwing and multi-discipline.

The first category incorporates the 100, 200 and 400 metres sprints and the 110 and 400 metres hurdles. Regarded as the most prestigious of Olympic athletic events, the winner of the 100 metres is usually considered to be the world's fastest man or woman. The profile of the 200 metres has increased considerably over recent years in part due to the phenomenal record breaking performance of Michael Johnson during the 1996 Atlanta Games. The 400 metres has always been considered a difficult race to run requiring immense tolerance to the build up of lactic acid – the substance that causes that heavy legged feeling during exercise. Many sprinters have combined the 100 and 200 metres or the 200 and 400 metres but very few are capable of contesting all three successfully.

Middle distance runners are not only required to be able to cover the ground at high speed, the must also be thinkers and tacticians. Whilst sprint races are run close to flat out for their entire distance,

LEFT Robert Korzeniowski of Poland competes in the men's 50 kilometre race walk en route to winning the gold medal during the Athens 2004 Olympic Games

Although dominated over many decades by athletes from Finland, Czechoslovakia and the Soviet Union, the long distance events have for some years been the showcase for the top athletes of the African nations. To run competitively at distances of 5,000 metres and over the athletes must posses an exceptional level of anaerobic conditioning and complete, uninterrupted mental determination to cope with the ever changing tactics and long periods of time spent pounding the track. In the words of the great Czech athlete Emile Zátopek, "If you want to win something, run the 100 metres. If you want to experience something, run the marathon."

A curious event exists in the form of the 20,000 and 50,000 metres walks. Competitors are required to keep at least one foot in contact with the ground at all times whilst ensuring that their leading leg remains straight at the point of first contact.

The jumping category incorporates the high, long and triple jumps in addition to the pole vault. Competitors in the high jump are allowed to choose the height at which their first attempt is made and are permitted three attempts to clear the bar. If an athlete fails to clear the bar they may

these events can be played out at almost any pace from the gun. Women's events above 400 metres were suspended from 1928 until the Games of 1960 because officials considered the exhaustion it caused the athletes to be unhealthy and dangerous. It is interesting to note that the current best women's 800 metres time would have been fast enough to have taken the bronze medal in the men's event at those 1928 Olympics.

ABOVE Mary Rand of
Great Britain in action
during the long jump
event at the Olympic
Games in Tokyo. She
finished with a world
record jump of
6.76metres to win the
Gold Medal

move on to the next height but three consecutive failures results in elimination.
Athletes in the long and triple jumps are
given three attempts to qualify for a final
field of twelve competitors. Should the
athlete launch their jump after the take-
off board, land outside the sand pit or
perform any sort of somersault a no-

jump is recorded. A triple jumper must
first land on his take-off foot then land
on his opposite foot before completing
the exercise with a jump landing two
footed in the pit.

The throwing events comprise of the
shot, discus, hammer and javelin. The
shot is an iron ball, 7.26 kilograms in
weight for men and 4 kilograms for
women, that is thrown from within a 2.1
metre shot circle. Each competitor is
given three throws to qualify for the final
in which the top eight athletes are given
three more attempts. The discus is the
only track and field event in whose world
record has not been beaten in Olympic
competition. The discus is 2 kilograms
in weight for men, half that for women,
and is thrown from within a 2.5 metre
circle The hammer is a 7.26 kilogram ball
attached to a handle by a 120 centimetre
steel wire. Throwers make three to four
full rotations with the 2.1 metre hammer
circle before launching the ball down the
course with an initial velocity in excess of
100 km/h. With all of these events competitors must stay within the circle when
executing their throw, exiting to the rear.
Failure to do so results in the attempt
being marked as a no-throw.

An Olympic javelin, its shaft con-

ABOVE Olga
Kuzenkova of Russia
competes in the
women's hammer throw
final during the Athens
2004 Olympic Games

structed of wood or metal, is 2.7 metres in length with a minimum weight of 800 grams. Throws are made from above the shoulder after a run up of up to 36 metres. For a throw to be declared valid its tip must break the surface of the ground on impact. In 1986 the world record distance for the javelin throw was reset after changes were implemented in the design of the javelin itself following a series of dangerously long throws.

There are two multi-sport events contested in Olympic competition. The men's decathlon comprises of the 100 metres sprint, long jump, shot put, high jump, 400 metres, 100 metres hurdles, discus, pole vault, javelin and 1500 metres whilst the women's heptathlon consists of a 100 metres hurdles, high jump, shot put, 200 metres, long jump, javelin and 800 metres. The rules used in each event are the same as those for the individual competitions with the exception that competitors are allowed two false starts instead of one. Points are awarded for each event based upon a series of tables approved by the International Amateur Athletics Federation.

Triathlon

TRIATHLON MADE ITS OLYMPIC debut on the first day of competition at the 2000 Sydney Games in front of a crowd of 200,000 spectators. The sport was invented in 1974 by members of the San Diego Track Club as an alternative to the monotony of track training. Their first event comprised a 10 kilometre run, an 8 kilometre cycle followed by a 500m swim.

The distances involved in the Olympic triathlon are somewhat greater. A 1,500 metre open water swim is followed by a 40 kilometres cycle and then a 10,000 metres run with men and women both competing over the same distances. With the clock running from start to finish time can often be made up by speedy changes between each element, known as transitions.

Triathletes must wear a coloured cap for identification in the swimming phase with the use of a wetsuit being dependent on water temperature. If the water is below 14°C then a wetsuit is mandatory, between 14°C and 20°C it is optional and over 20°C it is outlawed. During the cycling element the use of an approved helmet is compulsory.

Qualification for the Olympic triathlon is based upon the athlete's world ranking but is limited to a maximum of three competitors per nation for each of the men's and women's competitions.

Up and Over

FOR MANY YEARS THE TECHNIQUE of the high jump had been evolving. The early twentieth century had seen extensive use of the western roll developed by American George Horine in which the jumper approached at an angle, taking off on his inner leg to roll sideways over the bar. This method remained popular up until the Berlin Olympics of 1936.

From the 1948 Games competition had been dominated by American and Russian high jumpers with the evolution of the straddle jump in which the athlete rotated his torso around the bar as he rolled over it. The success of Ukrainian world record holder Valery Brumel in this technique saw American coaches travelling to Russia to learn from his coaches.

The 1968 a young American jumper, Dick Fosbury, made his Olympic debut. Practically unknown just a year before he set the games alight with his revolutionary "Fosbury flop". Approaching the bar at high speed, Fosbury took of on his inside leg just as everybody else but then rotated himself onto his back crossing the bar head first. Spectators, judges and coaches were amazed as this new star cleared every height through to 2.24 metres to take the Olympic gold medal.

Fosbury never repeated his gold medal glory but his name will live on for ever in Olympic History with the "Fosbury flop" now considered the standard technique.

BELOW Dick Fosbury of the USA clears the bar in the high jump competiton with his dramatic new jumping style

Virén

RIGHT Lasse Viren wins the 5,000-meter run during the Olympic Games held in Montreal

LASSE VIRÉN WAS A FLYING Finn in the tradition of Olympic greats Hannes Kolehmainen and Paavo Nurmi. A police officer by profession, Virén trained for countless hours in the forests that surrounded his home town of Myrskylä, Finland.

Virén's Olympic debut came in the 10,000 metres at the 1972 Munich Games. Briton David Bedford set off at a blistering world record pace. His strategy had been to blow apart the opposition but with 4,600 metres covered there were still eight runners with him including Virén. Disaster struck as the Finn stumbled and fell to the ground taking Mohamed Gammoudi of Tunisia with him. Quick to his feet, Virén was up to second place within 230 metres. The lead changed several times until with 600 metres to go Virén attacked. Nobody had the strength to go with him as he sprinted home to a gold medal and a new world record. Virén complemented his 10,000 metres victory with a gold medal and Olympic record in the 5,000 metres just days later to become only the fourth runner to achieve a 5,000 / 10,000 metres double.

A third gold medal was achieved four years later in the 10,000 metres at the Montreal Games. Portuguese athlete Carlos Lopes took on the field pulling away from all but Virén who unleashed his kick with 450 metres remaining to win the gold medal by 30 metres. Four days later Virén claimed his fourth Olympic gold taking victory in the 5,000 metres to become the first repeat winner of the event.

Weightlifting

WEIGHTLIFTING WAS INCLUDED IN the programme of the first Olympic Games in 1896 but was categorised as part of the athletics schedule. It was only in 1920 that it was classified as a sport in its own right. There have been many variations of the lifts required in Olympic competition. Early Olympic competition included one-handed lifts and a dumbbell event. Women's weightlifting was introduced to the Olympics at the 2000 Games.

The current weightlifting program requires the completion of two lifts – the snatch and the clean-and-jerk. In both phases the competitor chooses at which weight to commence lifting and the subsequent level of increase as the rounds progress and have three attempts at each lift. The competitor who lifts the highest combined weight for snatch and clean-and-jerk wins the competition. In the event of a tie the competitor with the lowest bodyweight wins.

To complete a snatch the competitor must lift the weight using a wide armed position in one movement from the floor to above his head and hold it still until a signal is given by the referee. The clean-and-jerk is a two stage lift in which the bar is held with arms at shoulder width. The bar is first drawn to the chest and then lifted to the full stretch of the arms over the competitors head.

ABOVE Action in the weightlifting competition in Athens 2004

XXX Olympiad

LONDON WILL HOST THE GAMES of the XXX Olympiad in the summer of 2012. Final selection was held during the 117th session of the International Olympic Committee at the Raffles City Convention Centre in Singapore on 6 July 2005. Of the five candidate cities, Moscow was the first to be eliminated from the voting followed by New York and Madrid. The final vote was between Paris and London with the French capital considered the favourite following its successful hosting of the 1998 FIFA World Cup Finals. With a majority of 54 votes to Paris' 50, London was announced as the host city of the 2012 Olympic Games.

BELOW The Olympic Evaluation Committee listen to a question from the media at Canary Wharf on the findings of their four day visit to assess the London bid for the 2012 Olympic Games

The 2012 Games will make use of a combination of new, existing and temporary venues that will mix modern developments with historical landmarks. Three zones have been created within the city – the Olympic Park Zone, the River Zone and the Central Zone with additional venues proposed across the nation.

The centre of activity will be the Olympic Park situated in Stratford, East London. This 500 acre site will provide a home for nine venues including the main 80,000 seat Olympic Stadium, the Aquatics Centre, Hockey Centre and Velopark in addition to four multi-sport arenas that will see events as diverse as volleyball, fencing, basketball and handball. The park will also house

CONGRATULATIONS

LONDON 2012

Lord's:
London's Olympic archery venue

natwest.com/cricket

the Olympic village providing accommodation for every competitor and team official, its location offering access to all venues within 20 minutes for 80 per cent of Olympic athletes and 95 per cent of Paralympic athletes.

The River Zone straddles the Thames to the east of the city. Many existing facilities will be put to use. North of the river the docklands based ExCel centre will provide a location for boxing, judo, table tennis, Taekwando, weightlifting and wrestling. To the south the ubiquitous "Millennium" Dome will rise like a phoenix to host the finals of the basketball, the rhythmic gymnastics and trampoline competition. The adjacent Greenwich Arena, a temporary facility, will be the venue for the rhythmic gymnastics and badminton events. A little to the south Greenwich Park, London's oldest Royal Park and home of the Royal Greenwich Observatory and the National Maritime Museum, will host the modern pentathlon and all the equestrian events whilst to the east the

Royal Artillery Barracks at Woolwich will house the shooting competitions.

The Central Zone is, not surprisingly, in the absolute heart of the city. London landmark Horse Guards Parade in Westminster will host the beach volleyball competition in a specially created arena whilst Lords, home of cricket, will become a home to archery. Hyde Park will provide an exciting venue for the triathlon with competitors performing their open water swim in the Serpentine before completing their cycling and running phases within the park grounds. To the north another of the Royal Parks, Regent's Park, will provide the start and finish of a demanding road cycling course that will send competitors up and around Hampstead Heath.

Outside of the three zones other events are scheduled making use of existing facilities. The unique All England Lawn Tennis and Croquet Club in Wimbledon will host an exciting tennis tournament. The recently finished Eton College Rowing Centre at Dorney, near Windsor, will be the venue for all rowing and flat-water canoe and kayak events with the slalom events being contested at Broxbourne on the edge of the Lea Valley Park in Hertfordshire.

Further afield, Glasgow's Hampden Park, Newcastle's St James' Park, Manchester's Old Trafford, Birmingham's Villa Park, the Cardiff Millennium Stadium and the newly built Wembley Stadium in London will host the football tournament. Weymouth and Portland on England's south west coast will provide an ideal venue for all classes of the sailing competitions.

It is estimated that the new venues will cost approximately £560 million with the Olympic Village costing an additional £65 million. On top of this £1.5 billion is budgeted for the actual running of the 2012 Games. Organisers expect 75 per cent of the 8 million available tickets, which will also offer free travel on London Transport, to be sold for under £50. A further 1.6 million tickets are to be made available for the Paralympic Games.

Public transport, an issue for which

London is often criticised, will undergo a programme of regeneration and upgrade with improvements to the Northern and East London Underground lines and the Docklands Light Railway. A new train service, the Olympic Javelin, is being constructed to provide a 140 mph rail link enabling passengers from central London and Dartford in Kent to access the Olympic Park quickly and efficiently.

ABOVE Construction work in Stratford, the site of the Olympic Park for the 2012 Olympics

LEFT An aerial view of the construction work for the London 2012 Olympic Games

Yifter

RIGHT Mirtus Yifter brushes shoulders with a competitor before passing him and claiming victory in the men's 5,000m at the 1980 Olympic Games in Moscow

ETHIOPIAN MIRUTS YIFTER was born in Adigrat, Tigray Province. Having spent time as a carriage driver, it was not until he joined the Ethiopian Air Force that his talent for running was discovered.

Yifter made his Olympic debut at the Munich Games of 1972 winning a bronze medal in the 10,000 metres behind the great Lasse Virén of Finland. However, arriving too late for the start of his heat he was eliminated from the 5,000 metres. It has since been suggested that as Yifter came from Tigray, a region involved in an uprising against the ruling dictatorship of Ethiopia, he had been intentionally misinformed by team officials preventing him from competing.

Restricted by the pan-African boycott of 1976, Yifter was unable to participate in Olympic competition again until the Moscow Games of 1980. The final of the 10,000 metres was dominated by the Ethiopian runners with only Virén and his Finnish team mate Maaninka staying in contention. With 300 metres remaining Yifter sprinted clear to take his first Olympic gold.

After his 1972 debacle he easily qualified for the 5,000 metres final. At 4,000 metres all twelve finalists were still together, Yifter apparently caught in the middle with countryman Mohammed Kadir in front of him. With only 300 metres to the finish, Kadir looked round and with the wave of a hand stepped aside allowing Yifter to unleash the sprint that had earned him the nickname "Yifter the Shifter". Powering away he crossed the line first to take the gold medal that had eluded him eight years before.

Zátopek

A CARPENTER'S SON, EMIL ZÁTOPEK was born in Koprivince, Czechoslovakia in 1922. Joining the army in 1944, his athletic prowess was noted and encouraged and a young lieutenant Zátopek was sent to the 1948 London Olympics.

Viljo Heino was expected to take victory in the 10,000 metres but a ferocious pace set by Zátopek forced the Finn to drop out from exhaustion. Zátopek lapped all but two runners to take the gold medal. Three days later he competed in the 5,000 metres final securing a silver medal.

Zátopek's greatest achievements occurred at the 1952 Helsinki Olympics. Psychologically he won the 10,000 metres before it started, the other competitors standing back allowing him to choose his place on the line. Zátopek set the pace forcing his opponents into submission until he was on his own, a gold medal won.

Four days later in the closing laps of the 10,000 metres final a fierce battle ensued between Zátopek and three other athletes. Attacking on the final bend he powered away to take his second gold medal of the games. On that same day his wife, Dana, won a gold medal in the javelin.

Never having run the distance, Zátopek announced he would enter the marathon. Unsure about pace he decided to run alongside record holding Briton Jim Peters. 15 kilometres into the race Peters, Zátopek and Swede Gustav Jansson held a formidable lead. Looking across at Peters he asked if the pace was good enough. An exhausted Peters, trying to save face, replied "too slow". A few yards further Zátopek accelerated leaving Peters behind. Jansson faded after 20 miles but Zátopek pressed on alone to finish two-and-a-half minutes clear of the field. Zátopek had achieved an amazing Olympic treble.

ABOVE Emil Zátopek leads in front of French Alain Mimoun and Herbert Schade during the Olympic 5000m in Helsinki

Also available on DVD

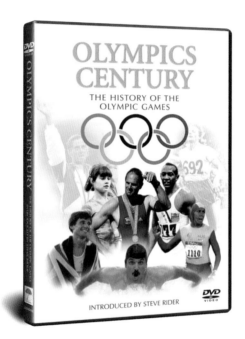

Available from all major stockists of DVDs or online at:
www.greenumbrellashop.co.uk

The pictures in this book were provided courtesy of the following:

GETTY IMAGES
101 Bayham Street, London NW1 0AG

Book design and artwork by Newleaf Design

Published by Green Umbrella

Series Editors Jules Gammond, Tim Exell, Vanessa Gardner

Written by Jon Stroud

Picture Research by Jon Stroud and Ellie Charleston